Gra
COMMON

The Sterling Book of Common Errors in English is designed to satisfy the needs of the mature student or user of the English language who desires to improve his English and acquire mastery of the language to achieve his particular aims in his academic, professional, political or social life.

It is not a textbook of grammar with its drab definitions and tedious sets of rules. It mostly deals with faculty expressions heard in everyday conversation. An easy-to-follow guide, it should help the reader to improve his language skills.

The book is the outcome of long years of teaching, keen observation and extensive research on common errors in grammar, punctuation and spelling.

The approach is simple—to identify as many common errors as possible. Some of them can be weeded out easily, others may need determined effort.

Mr. Gratian Vas has a Master of Arts degree in English Literature and has been in the field of education for the past few years.

BOOKS IN ENGLISH LANGUAGE LEARNING SERIES

Grammer Matters

Common Errors in English
Dictionary for Misspellers
Idioms
Quotations
Proverbs
Riddles
Tongue Twisters

The Complete Guide to

Business Letters
Effective English Writing
Essays for Competitive Examinations
Functional Writing in English
Modern Essays
Paragraph to Essay Writing
Prose Compositions
Résumé Writing
Letters for Social Interaction

Enrich your Grammar

Antonyms
Current Words and Phrases
Prepositions
Synonyms
Word Perfect
Word Power
Word to Paragraph
Words and Their Usages
Word Origins

Communications Skills

The Power of Spoken English (with 2 audio CDs)
Speaking and Writing in English
Dynamic Reading Skills
Effective Communication
English Conversation Practice
How to Develop Profitable Listening Skills
How to Increase Your Reading Speed
How to Listen Better
How to Read Effectively and Efficiently
How to Resolve Conflicts

Grammar Matters
COMMON ERRORS IN ENGLISH

GRATIAN VAS

STERLING PAPERBACKS
An imprint of
Sterling Publishers (P) Ltd.
A-59, Okhla Industrial Area, Phase-II,
New Delhi-110020.
Tel: 26387070, 26386209; Fax: 91-11-26383788
E-mail: mail@sterlingpublishers.com
www.sterlingpublishers.com

Common Errors in English
© 2006, Sterling Publishers Pvt. Ltd.
ISBN 978 81 207 1729 9
Reprint 2007, 2008, 2010, 2011, 2012, 2013

All rights are reserved.
No part of this publication may be reproduced, stored in a retrieval system or transmitted, in any form or by any means, mechanical, photocopying, recording or otherwise, without prior written permission of the original publisher.

Printed in India
Printed and Published by **Sterling Publishers Pvt. Ltd.,**
New Delhi-110 020.

PREFACE

A good grasp of grammar and a reasonably wide vocabulary are of much importance in effective communication through speech and writing. It is a skill that can be acquired by learning and practice.

This is a book on common mistakes in English, those committed not only by students in the classroom but by almost all who have learnt it as a second language. It is not a textbook of grammar with its drab definitions and tedious sets of rules. It mostly deals with faculty expressions heard in everyday conversation. An easy-to-follow guide, it should help the reader to improve his language skills.

The book is the outcome of long years of teaching, keen observation and extensive research on common mistakes in grammar, punctuation and spelling.

The approach is simple—to identify as many common mistakes as possible. Some of them can be weeded out easily, others may need determined effort.

Gratian Vas

CONTENTS

1. Nouns and Noun-phrases — 1
2. Pronouns — 9
3. Adjectives — 16
4. Verbs — 23
5. 'Will', 'Shall', 'Would' and 'Should' — 34
6. Adverbs — 37
7. Prepositions — 44
8. Conjunctions — 62
9. Sequence of Tenses — 70
10. Articles — 74
11. Singular and Plural Numbers — 84
12. Gender — 89
13. Proverbs — 91
14. Spelling — 97
15. Words Commonly Confused — 124
16. Inappropriate Use of Words — 136
17. Punctuation — 142
18. Other Mistakes — 150

NOUNS AND NOUN PHRASES

INCORRECT	CORRECT
1. We have received no *informations*.	We have received no *information*.
2. *Politics are* not meant for me.	*Politics is* not meant for me.
3. He was troubled by *these news*.	He was troubled by *this news*.
4. We saw beautiful *sceneries* in Kashmir.	We saw beautiful *scenery* in Kashmir.
5. I will take care of your *luggages*.	I will take care of your *luggage*.
6. *Gymnastics are* given a lot of importance in our school.	*Gymnastics is* given a lot of importance in our school.
7. There were no *breads* in the shop.	There was no *bread* in the shop. or There were no loaves of bread in the shop.
8. We have bought some new *furnitures*.	We have bought some new *furniture*.
9. Please excuse the *troubles*.	Please excuse me for the *trouble*.
10. The *blinds* need our support.	The *blind* need our support.
11. He was overcome by the misery of the *poors*.	He was overcome by the misery of the *poor*.

INCORRECT	CORRECT
12. The *cattles* are a nuisance on our streets.	The *cattle* are a nuisance on our streets.
13. I have had my *meals*.	I have had my *meal*.
14. My *family members* will join me soon.	The *members of my family* will join me soon. or My *family* will join me soon.
15. He had been to his *mother's-in-law* house.	He had been to his *mother-in-law's* house.
16. Her *hairs* are brown.	Her *hair* is brown.
17. She is good at *Mathematic*.	She is good at *Mathematics*.
18. He has received his *transfer order*.	He has received his *transfer orders*.
19. *Summons have* been served on the defaulters.	*Summons has* been served on the defaulters.
20. I have come to pay my *respect* to my teacher.	I have come to pay my *respects* to my teacher.
21. He has received only a *two-third* of his pay.	He has received only a *two-thirds* of his pay.
22. He brought me three *dozens* oranges.	He brought me three *dozen* oranges.
23. He is a good *neighbourer*.	He is a good *neighbour*.
24. There is no *place* in this compartment.	There is no *room* in this compartment.
25. My sister is taking part in *the drama*.	My sister is taking part in *the play*.
26. We had a good *play* of cricket.	We had a good *game* of cricket.
27. There were *jokers* at the circus.	There were *clowns* at the circus.
28. We have been asked to memorize the *poetry*.	We have been asked to memorize the *poem*.

	INCORRECT	CORRECT
29.	She came to his *boarding*.	She came to his *boarding house*.
30.	He asked me for a piece of *blotting*.	He asked me for a piece of *blotting paper*.
31.	He was writing it out in his *copy*.	He was writing it out in his *notebook*.
32.	They had only two *waiting members* in their team.	They had only two *reserves* in their team.
33.	This is the fruit of my father's good *advices*.	This is the fruit of my father's good *advice*.
34.	*Athletics are* his favourite sport.	*Athletics is* his favourite sport.
35.	She forgot to bring her *scissor*.	She forgot to bring her *scissors*.
36.	You must start eating *fruits* daily.	You must start eating *fruit* daily.
37.	I have been advised to eat a lot of green *vegetables*.	I have been advised to eat a lot of green *vegetable*.
38.	My grandmother does not wear *spectacle*.	My grandmother does not wear *spectacles*.
39.	He is a supporter of land *reform*.	He is a supporter of land *reforms*.
40.	He forgot to wash his *trouser*.	He forgot to wash his *trousers*.
41.	The gentry of the town *was* present to greet him.	The gentry of the town *were* present to greet him.
42.	I saw two *females* at the party.	I saw two *ladies/women* at the party.
43.	She has got into bad *companionship*.	She has got into had *company*.
44.	He spent a large *number* of money at the fair.	He spent a large *amount* of money at the fair.
45.	The man wore new *dress*.	The man wore new *clothes*.

INCORRECT	CORRECT
46. He forgot to put down his *sign* on the application.	He forgot to put down his *signature* on the application.
47. She is my *cousin sister*.	She is my *cousin*.
48. She took *insult* at my remark.	She took *offence* at my remark.
49. We are all *fellow brothers*.	We are all *brothers*.
50. Delhi is one of the most polluted *city* in the world.	Delhi is one of the most polluted *cities* in the world.
51. The road is closed for *repair*.	The road is closed for *repairs*.
52. One of my *student* has won the gold medal for public speaking.	One of my *students* has won the gold for public speaking.
53. Don't look at the *back side* of my house.	Don't took at the *back* of my house.
54. She happened to hurt a *foot finger*.	She happened to hurt a *toe*.
55. He has a ten-*rupees* note.	He has a ten-*rupee* note.
56. There are two ladies *in* our staff.	There are two ladies *on* our staff.
57. He *has* a Ph.D. in English.	He *is* a Ph.D. in English.
58. I think the *chair's legs* are broken.	I think the *legs of the chair* are broken.
59. *Good night*. I'm happy you could come.	*Good evening*. I'm happy you could come.
60. Cloth is sold by the *yards*.	Cloth is sold by the *yard*.
61. He sees that *alms is* given to every beggar that comes to his door.	He sees that *alms are* given to every beggar that comes to his door.
62. I'm leaving by the *8.00* train.	I'm leaving by the *8 o'clock* train.
63. I expect you to be true to your *words*.	I expect you to be true to your *word*.

	INCORRECT	CORRECT
64.	I have *works* to do in the city.	I have *much work* to do in the city.
65.	He has no *issues* other than a daughter.	He has no *issue* other than a daughter.
66.	The new *machineries have* arrived.	The new *machinery has* arrived.
67.	I found him sleeping in his *quarter*.	I found him sleeping in his *quarters*.
68.	It is bad *manner* to eavesdrop.	It is bad *manners* to eavesdrop.
69.	You will be surprised at your own *emolument*.	You will be surprised at your own *emoluments*.
70.	Take a *compass* and draw a circle.	Take the *compasses* and draw a circle.
71.	I must change my *cloths* immediately.	I must change my *clothes* immediately.
72.	You have always been finding *faults* with my work.	You have always been finding *fault* with my work.
73.	You need not worry yourself about the *finance* of the company.	You need not worry yourself about the *finances* of the company.
74.	He has gone abroad for higher *study*.	He has gone abroad for higher *studies*.
75.	He has got this job on *merits*.	He has got this job on *merit*.
76.	The course *materials* you sent were very useful.	The course *material* you sent was very useful.
77.	My *circumstance* does not permit me to leave home at this stage.	My *circumstances* do not permit me to leave home at this stage.
78.	The police *was* late in coming.	The police *were* late in coming.
79.	A *ten-men* delegation met the chairman.	A *ten-man* delegation met the chairman.

INCORRECT	CORRECT
80. Where are you going to spend your summer *vacations* this year?	Where are you going to spend your summer *vacation* this year?
81. The earthquake has caused *many* damages.	The earthquake has caused *much* damage.
82. He met all my *fooding* expenses.	He met all my *food* expenses.
83. The *sister of my friend* came to see me.	*My friend's sister* came to see me.
84. He is too fond of his *offsprings*.	He is too fond of his *offspring*.
85. The *hall's walls* need to be painted.	The *walls of the hall* need to be painted.
86. Please sanction me one *day* leave.	Please sanction me one *day's* leave.
87. The *weather* at the hill resort was fine.	The *climate* at the hill resort was fine.

☞ NOTES

1. 'Rices', 'corns', 'foods' are used to denote different kinds of rice, corn, food and not a large quantity of these items. Similarly 'advice', 'scenery', 'hair', 'offspring', 'furniture', etc., do not take 's' after them unless the other meaning of the word is intended. 'Advice' means counsel, but 'advices' means information, 'sceneries' denote different kinds of scenery. 'Hairs' is used when attention is drawn to number. 'Abuses' denotes evil practices and is not a term of abuse.

2. The following nouns are alike in the singular and the plural: 'fish', 'deer', 'sheep', 'pice', 'trout', 'cod', 'salmon', 'species', 'canon', 'urine', 'series', 'corps', etc.

3. The following nouns are always used in the plural: 'shoes', 'socks', 'bellows', 'tongs', 'precincts', 'trousers', 'stockings', 'spectacles', 'scissors', 'fetters', 'shears', 'cards', 'pants', 'pyjamas', 'glanders', 'billiards', 'bowels', 'draughts', 'thanks', 'annals', 'entrails', 'contents', 'savings', 'remains', proceeds', 'lodgings', 'auspices', 'premises', 'assets', 'victuals', 'aims', 'riches', 'ashes', 'cares', 'nuptials', 'innings',

'quarters', 'wages', 'breeches', 'surroundings', 'tactics', 'dregs', 'eaves', 'pincers', and 'letters'.
4. The following nouns are plural in form, but are used as singular: 'alms', 'runnings', 'gallows', 'news', 'amends', 'Politics', 'Ethics', 'Mathematics', 'Dynamics', 'Physics', 'Gymnastics', 'means' (meaning wealth), 'summons', (the plural is 'summonses').
5. Nouns expressing number and weight (when preceded by numerals) are not pluralised, as : 'five dozen apples'; 'two score mangoes'; twelve stone weight, 'five head of cattle', 'two hundred rupees', three thousand rupees', four yoke of oxen', 'a five-yard piece of cloth, 'a three-mile race', etc.
But we say: 'There were thousands of people in the fair'. 'Hundreds of boys came to watch the match'.
6. 'Politics', 'Mechanics', 'Optics', 'Mathematics', 'Gymnastics', 'Physics', etc. - These words always take an 's' after them, but they take singular verbs.
7. There are other nouns that always take a plural form and a plural verb.
8. Some nouns have the same form in the singular as well as in the plural, e.g.: 'swine', 'sheep', 'grass', 'score', 'fish', 'salmon', 'canon', etc.
9. Certain collective nouns preceded by a numeral do not take an 's' after them, e.g., 'many counsel'
10. Collective nouns like 'dozen' and pair', though singlular in form, are always used in the plural: (1) My poultry have made me rich. (2) The people of our village are rich. (3) The cattle are grazing. (4) Mankind want peace. (5) The gentry have been invited. (6) The vermin are killed. (7) The peasantry of India are industrious. (8) The police were sent on the track. (9) The clergy were present.
11. When 'people' is used as a common noun, it is used both in the singular and in the plural. The Nepalese are a simple and brave people. The peoples (nations) of Africa are making rapid progress.
12. Abstract, proper and material nouns have no plural except when they are used as common nouns.
13. When a noun is made to do the work of an adjective in a compound word, it should not be used in the plural form: 'a ten-rupee note', 'a hundred-yard race', 'a ten-year-old boy', a two-hour talk', 'an eight-anna piece', a five-year plan', 'a ten-pound weight', a 'seven-day week', 'a 'three-hour talk', etc.
We say 'pieces of art', 'pieces of poetry', 'pieces of advice' and

'articles of clothing', 'articles of furniture', 'articles of baggage'. 'Fishes' denotes different kinds of fish; 'hairs', different kinds of hair.
14. Some nouns have two forms in the plural, each with a different meaning.
15. The apostrophe 's' after a noun is added only in the case of animate objects, not in the case of inanimate ones, except after expressions which denote: (i) time; (ii) weight; (iii) distance, e.g. : 'a maund's weight', 'a mile's distance', 'an hour's talk', 'a stone's throw', 'a needle's point', 'a week's leave', etc.
16. The words 'church', 'school', 'house', 'shop', etc., are often omitted after the possessive case.
17. Avoid use of the double possessive, e.g., your's.
18. The words, 'its', 'his', 'hers', 'yours', 'ours', and 'theirs', are possessive. They are neither written within the possessive sign (') nor are followed by nouns.
19. In plural nouns ending in 's', possessive case is formed by adding a single apostrophe after the 's', e.g.: girls' colleges', boys', schools'.
20. In plural nouns not ending in 's', the possessive case is formed by adding an apostrophe before the 's', e.g:, children's park, men's club, and women's hostel.
21. To change a plural noun into the possessive case remember that
    a) If it denotes persons ('men', 'ladies',) and does not end in 's', an apostrophe is added before the 's' e.g. 'Children's books'; 'men's' garments'; etc.
    b) Nouns denoting objects also take an apostrophe before the 's', e.g. : 'Death's toll', 'life's burden', 'India's heroes'.
    c) Apostrophes are also used in the following familiar phrases: 'Out of harm's way', 'to his heart's content', 'at his wit's end', 'a bird's-eye view,'
    d) In plural nouns ending in (s) a single apostrophe is used after the 's', e.g., girls' college', 'boys' school', 'for goodness' sake', 'Moses' Law'.

2
PRONOUNS

INCORRECT	CORRECT
1. Each of the directors *dislike* the new managing director.	Each of the directors *dislikes* the new managing director.
2. *Both did not* take part in the discussions.	*Neither* took part in the discussions.
3. *We all did not* participate in the seminar.	*None* of us participated in the seminar.
4. Let Priya and *I* go home.	Let Priya and *me* go home.
5. I will take *your leave* after two hours.	I will take *leave of you* after two hours.
6. You played better than *me*.	You played better than *I*.
7. This job cannot be entrusted to anyone except *he*.	This job cannot be entrusted to anyone except *him*.
8. None of them *were* here.	None of them *was* here.
9. *Our's* is a small company.	*Ours* is a small company.
10. Radha *keeps herself away* from late night parties.	Radha *keeps away* from late night parties.
11. It was *me* who picked up your father last night.	It was *I* who picked up your father last night.
12. That is my book; please *pass*.	That is my book; please *pass it*.

INCORRECT	CORRECT
13. I asked the boss for a raise in pay but he did not *give me*.	I asked the boss for a raise in pay but he did not *give it to me*.
14. *I* and *she* are friends.	*She* and *I* are friends.
15. The man who comes here *first he will* get the job.	The man who comes here *first will* get the job.
16. Whoever tops the class *she will* be selected.	Whoever tops the class *will* be selected.
17. I with some colleagues attended the conference.	I attended the conference with some colleagues.
18. The chairman examined the candidate if he was fit for the job.	The chairman examined the candidate to see if he was fit for the job.
19. Have you a pen? I have not *got*.	Have you a pen? I have not got one.
20. Is he at home? Yes, I *think*.	Is he at home? Yes, I *think so*.
21. Who did this? *Myself*.	Who did this? *I* (Myself).
22. They *enjoyed* during holidays.	They *enjoyed themselves* during holidays.
23. *Any* of these two girls will be sent for training.	*Either* of these girls will be sent for training.
24. There is no choice between you and *she*.	There is no choice between you and *her*.
25. Neither the station master nor his subordinates was present at *his* station.	Neither the station master nor his subordinates were present at *their* station.
26. I saw every woman and every girl raise *their* hands.	I saw every woman and every girl raise *her* hands.

INCORRECT	CORRECT
27. The principal found each master and each boy in *their* rooms.	The principal found each master and each boy in *his* room.
28. I shall check the switches *whether they* work.	I shall check whether the *switches* work.
29. Everyone is sad when *they see* little children exploited.	Everyone is sad when *he sees* little children exploited.
30. None of us *have* seen him for quite some time now.	None of us *has* seen him for quite some time now.
31. The size of the bracelet should be the same *as this* bracelet.	The size of the bracelet should be the same *as that of this* bracelet.
32. My car is more expensive than *my friend's*.	My car is more expensive than *that of my friend*.
33. *I, you and she* are expected to attend the seminar.	*You, she and I* are expected to attend the seminar.
34. You and I have done *my* work.	You and I have done *our* work.
35. You and he tried *his* best to convince her of her responsibility.	You and he tried *your* best to convince her of her responsibility.
36. Let you and *I* handle this job together.	Let you and *me* handle this job together.
37. If I were *him,* I would have resigned.	If I were *he,* I would have resigned.
38. Will you accept *either of* these five proposals?	Will you accept *any of* these five proposals
39. Percy and Nina love *one* another.	Percy and Nina love *each* other.
40. All the officers should respect *each other*.	All the officers should respect *one another*.
41. One should respect *his* parents at all times.	One should respect *one's* parents at all time.

INCORRECT	CORRECT
42. Everyone collected *one's* pay on the first.	Everyone collected *his* pay on the first.
43. Every one of us should be faithful to *their* organisation.	Every one of us should be faithful to *his* organisation.
44. Such persons *who* are diligent, achieve success in life.	Such persons *as* are diligent, achieve success in life.
45. This is the same man *whom* you met yesterday.	This is the same man *who* you met yesterday.
46. *Whom* do you suspect has done this?	*Who* do you suspect has done this?
47. You should avail of *this* opportunity to go abroad.	You should avail *yourself* of this opportunity to go abroad.
48. Who is there? It is *me*.	Who is there? It is *I*.
49. The teacher has helped Rita and *I*.	The teacher has helped Rita and *me*.
50. Anika sings better than *me*.	Anika sings better than *I (do)*.
51. You are as good a player as *him*.	You are as good a player as *he*.
52. Have you any objection to *I* joining you on this trip?	Have you any objection to *me* joining you on this trip?
53. *Your's* sincerely.	*Yours* sincerely.
54. He is not such a fool *that* would resign.	He is not such a fool *as* would resign.
55. Those who attended this discussion should consider *yourself* fortunate.	Those who attended this discussion should consider *themselves* fortunate.
56. Which of you would like to lend Asif *your* book?	Which of you would like to lend Asif *his* book?
57. He is the best defender *who* could be found.	He is the best defender *that* could be found.

	INCORRECT	CORRECT
58.	This is between *you* and *I*.	This is between *you* and *me*.
59.	She went with Gita and *myself*.	She went with Gita and *me*.
60.	*Who* did you see at the fair?	*Whom* did you see at the fair?
61.	This is the same table *whose leg* you had broken.	This the same table *the leg of which* you had broken.
62.	It was *him* who did it.	It was *he* who did it.
63.	He *made your mention* in his talk.	He *made a mention of you* in his talk.
64.	I was pleased to receive *your good report*.	I was pleased to receive *a good report of you*.
65.	I am *yours* obedient servant.	I am *your* obedient servant.
66.	I have read *Browning's poetry* who was a lover of nature.	I have read *the poetry of Browning* who was a lover of nature.
67.	It is the system, not the individual, which he hates.	It is the system which he hates, not the individual.
68.	He repeated the story to *whoever* he met.	He repeated the story to *whomsoever* he met.
69.	I am happy at *them* taking part in this competition.	I am happy at *their* taking part in this competition.
70.	All but *him* had passed.	All but *he* had passed.

☞ NOTES

1. 'I' comes last, when 'you' and 'he' are mentioned in the same sentence, but in admitting a fault, 'I' comes first.
2. 'Which' conveys additional information, somewhat new, and 'that' merely explains and defines a certain thing or statement.
3. The vernacular idiom is responsible for the mistakes in sentences such as: She *enjoyed* during her holidays.
4. A pronoun used as subject should not be separated from its verb if possible.
5. 'Each', 'every', 'none', 'person', 'much', are singular words, 'many', 'all', 'most', 'some', 'people' are plurals.

6. 'Either' is used for two things, 'any' is used for more than two.
7. The relative pronoun should be placed as near as possible to its antecedent, so that no ambiguity may arise.
8. When two or more singular nouns are joined by either ... or, neither ... nor, the pronouns are generally used in the singular.
9. When two singular nouns joined by 'and' are preceded by 'each' or 'every', the pronoun used for them is in the singular.
10. If a plural and a singular noun are joined by either ... or, neither ... nor, the pronoun and verb used should be in the plural.
11. When pronouns of different persons are joined by 'and' and used as the subject of a sentence, the verb is used in the plural.
12. When there are pronouns of different persons, second person should come first, third person next and first person last, unless used in a pejorative sense when the order is reversed.
13. 'None' is used in the singular when it points to a material noun, e.g.: 'I want some flour, there is none in the bag.'
    'None' is used in the singular or the plural form when it points to persons or common nouns; e.g.: 'Is there any message for me?' 'No, there is none' (singular). 'None but the hard working deserve the award.' 'Do you want apples?' 'There are none in the basket.'
14. Pronouns like 'his', 'her' are used for 'each', and 'everyone', according to reference.
15. When the gender (masculine or feminine) is not expressed, 'he' is used.
16. The relative pronoun is sometimes omitted in the objective case.
17. The antecedent of a relative pronoun is sometimes omitted.
18. A relative pronoun should agree with its antecedent in number and person.
19. Generally 'whose' is used for denoting persons, and 'which' for denoting lifeless objects.
20. Sometimes the pronoun 'it' is omitted, where it is needed.
21. 'Who' denotes subject and 'whom' stands for object.
22. The object of a verb or of a preposition, when it is a pronoun, should be in the objective form.
23. When such verbs as 'avail', 'absent', 'enjoy', 'apply', 'resign', 'drink', 'acquit', 'over-reach', 'exert', 'oversleep', 'revenge', 'set', 'distinguish' are used reflexively, never omit the reflexive pronoun.
24. The complement of the verb 'to be', when it is expressed by a pronoun, should be in the nominative form.
25. The verbs 'break', 'enlist', 'bathe', 'qualify', 'dash', 'rest', 'keep', 'draw', 'move', 'roll', 'make', 'burst', 'spread', 'feel', 'lengthen', 'hide',

'marry', 'form', 'open', 'gather', 'steal', 'repent', 'stop' are not followed by reflexive pronouns.
26. A pronoun which is governed by a preposition must be in the objective case. Hence 'whom'.
27. A pronoun should not be omitted when it takes the place of a noun in the objective case after a transitive verb.
28. A noun or pronoun in the possessive case should not be used as the antecedent to a relative pronoun.
29. When a pronoun follows 'than' the case of such a pronoun is to be determined from the content.
30. Either use 'both' or 'as well as'.
31. Two singular subjects joined by as well as' require the a predicate verb to be singular.
32. When any two subjects, not of the same person, are joined by 'or' or 'nor', the verb agrees with the subject nearest it,
33. Singular subjects connected by 'or' or 'nor' need a singular verb.
34. In using 'neither', 'either', the verb should follow the second noun or pronoun.
35. A noun or pronoun in the possessive case should not be used as the antecedent to a relative pronoun.
36. A relative pronoun or the relative adverb should be placed as close to its antecedent as possible.
37. When a pronoun follows, then the case of such a pronoun is to be determined from the contents.
38. A noun or pronoun governing a gerund should be put in the possessive case. None should be put with 's'.
39. A noun or pronoun denoting a person or some other living being must be in the possessive case when placed before a gerund.

ADJECTIVES

INCORRECT	CORRECT
1. You have been working *hardly*.	You have been working *hard*.
2. Your flowers smell *sweetly*.	Your flowers smell *sweet*.
3. He arrived late as *usually*.	He arrived late as *usual*.
4. *Every people* come here for a good bargain.	*Everyone* comes here for a good bargain.
5. *These* all men are poor.	*All these* men are poor.
6. She held me *in the both hands*.	She held me *in both hands*. or She held me *in both her hands*.
7. She lives alone; she has *no any* children.	She lives alone, she has *no* children.
8. *Both servants* have not come today.	*Neither* servant has come today.
9. Don't sit idle, you must do *some or other work*.	Don't sit idle; you must do *some work or other*.
10. Sachin is greater than any other *cricketers*.	Sachin is greater than any other *cricketer*.
11. Open your book *at ten page*.	Open your book *at page ten*.
12. She is in *class fifth*.	She is *in class five*. or She is *in the fifth class*.

	INCORRECT	CORRECT
13.	I paid him *rupees fifty*.	I paid him *fifty rupees*.
14.	This coin belongs to the period of *King Charles the eighth*.	This coin belongs of the period of *King Charles VIII*.
15.	My sister is *elder* than I.	My sister is *older* than I.
16.	She sings *more better* than her sister.	She sings *better* than her sister.
17.	The son is *worst* than his father.	The son is *worse* than his father.
18.	Bombay is *dirty* than New Delhi.	Bombay is *dirtier* than New Delhi.
19.	A two-wheeler is *usefuller* than a car in our city.	A two-wheeler is *more useful* than a car in our city.
20.	He can't afford a house of his own because he gets *less* salary.	He can't afford a house of his own because he gets a *small* salary.
21.	In our company the number of workers is *less*.	In our company the number of workers is *small*.
22.	From the two the younger one is *smart*.	The younger one is the *smarter* of the two.
23.	Of the two stories this is the *best*.	Of the two stories this is the *better*.
24.	She is becoming *smart*.	She is becoming *smarter*.
25.	There is a *best* player in that team.	There is a very *good* player in that team.
26.	She has decided to spend *her remaining* life here.	She has decided to spend the *rest of her* life here.
27.	That was a *worth seeing* play.	That was a play *worth seeing*.
28.	There are no *less than* ten ladies here.	There are no *fewer* than ten ladies here.

	INCORRECT	CORRECT
29.	Romi is *most* generous and kinder than her sister.	Romi is *more* generous and kinder than her sister.
30.	*Each* participant cannot hope to win a gold medal.	*Every* participant cannot hope to win a gold medal.
31.	Ali is *wiser* than cunning.	Ali is *more wise* than cunning.
32.	He has not written *much* stories.	He has not written *many* stories.
33.	That parcel was *too much* heavy for her.	That parcel was *much too* heavy for her.
34.	Sharmila is the *most cleverest* girl in our class.	Sharmila is the *cleverest* girl in our class.
35.	Asha was the best and *famous* artist in this city.	Asha was the best and the *most famous* artist in this city.
36.	This is the strongest of *all other* metals.	This is the strongest of *all* metals.
37.	Milk is more useful than *any* food.	Milk is more useful than *any other* food.
38.	Tom's service is *more superior than* that of Trevor.	Tom's service is *superior* to that of Trevor.
39.	Many an artist *were* present at the gathering.	Many an artist *was* present at the gathering.
40.	*Whole the city* was present at his funeral.	*The whole city* was present at his funeral.
41.	*The all* participants were given certificates.	*All the* participants were given certificates.
42.	He has been helping the *blinds*.	He has been helping the *blind*.
43.	He has not taken *some* books from the library.	He has not taken *any* book from the library.
44.	Kapil is the *eldest* player on our side.	Kapil is the *oldest* player on our side.

INCORRECT	CORRECT
45. Gita had leave of *ten days*.	Gita had *ten days* leave. or Gita had leave *for ten days*.
46. *I'm hopeless* about our success.	*I have no hop*e of our success.
47. I have not seen a *so intelligent* dog.	I have not seen *so intelligent a dog*.
48. She was *so fat woman* that she could not pass through the door.	She was *so fat a woman* that she could not pass through the door.
49. *Yours* affectionate son.	*Your* affectionate son. or *Yours* affectionately.
50. Your *lovely* friend.	Your *loving* friend. or Yours *lovingly*.
51. I was surprised to see the *plain* countryside.	I was surprised to see the *flat* countryside.
52. We live *in hill* area.	We live *in a hill* area.
53. You *are coward*.	You *are a coward*.
54. Sheila can run *as fast, if not faster than you*.	Sheila can run *as fast as you, if not faster*.
55. Bangalore is *further* from Bombay than Pune.	Bangalore is *farther* from Bombay than Pune.
56. Roshan is brighter than *any boy* in his class.	Roshan is brighter than *any other boy* in his class.
57. *Each and every* student in the class got punished.	*Every* student in the class got punished.
58. Is the film festival commencing on *next Friday*?	Is the film festival commencing on *Friday next*?
59. She prefers milk *than* tea.	She prefers milk *to* tea.

INCORRECT	CORRECT
60. She is wiser than *all* students.	She is wiser than *all other* students.
61. Walking is *more preferable* to travelling in a bus here.	Walking is *preferable* to travelling in a bus here.
62. He gets just *passing* marks in English.	He gets just *pass* marks in English.
63. A *faithful servant* to his master is to be rewarded.	A *servant faithful* to his master should be rewarded.
64. The rain is *plenty* on the west.	The rain is *plentiful* on the west coast.
65. The *two first* chapters are the best in her book.	The *first two* chapters are the best in her book.
66. He did not make any *farther* remark.	He did not make any *further* remark.
67. *All the* class was absent.	*The whole* class was absent.
68. He is *best* player in our college.	He is *the best* player in our college.
69. I found *hundred* rupees under the table.	I found *hundred* rupees under the table.
70. I have *an urgent* business at the office.	I have *urgent* business (or some urgent business) at the office.
71. If you wish to hear what he says you should not make *noise*.	If you wish to hear what he says you should not make *a noise*.
72. *Himalayas* form the northern boundary of India.	*The Himalayas* form the northern boundary of India.
73. He hails from *the* Uttar Pradesh.	He hails *from* Uttar Pradesh.
74. You know Bombay *is big* city.	You know Bombay *is a big* city.
75. I mean *Hyderabad* in India.	I mean *the Hyderabad* in India.
76. *The diamonds* are forever.	*Diamonds* are forever.

INCORRECT	CORRECT
77. *The gold* is a precious metal.	*Gold* is a precious metal.
78. Man is a member of *the society*.	Man is a member *of society*.
79. We should love *the nature*.	We should *love nature*.
80. *The mankind* cannot ignore environment.	*Mankind* cannot ignore environment.
81. He has no love for *the God*.	He has no love for *God*.
82. He has reverence for all *gods* of Hinduism.	He has reverence for all *the gods* of Hinduism.
83. What *a fun!* Tomorrow is declared a holiday.	What *fun!* Tomorrow is declared a holiday.
84. *Ganges* is an important river.	*The Ganges* is an important river.
85. He went for *picnic* yesterday.	We went for *a picnic* yesterday.
86. *Much efforts* have brought their reward.	*Much effort* has brought its reward.
87. He is a *miser* man.	He is a *miserly* man.
88. He demanded a *sifting* inquiry.	He demanded a *thorough* inquiry.
89. I found the dog *laming*.	I found the dog *lame*.

☞ **NOTES**

1. Double comparative is wrong,
2. Comparatives ending in -'ior'- take 'to' and not 'than' after them.
3. 'Either' and 'neither' are used for two objects.
4. When 'that' and 'this', 'latter' and 'former', 'one' and 'other' refer to two objects previously mentioned, 'this', 'one', 'latter', refer to the second of them, and that 'other' and 'former' refer to the first.
5. When an adjective is connected with other words, it comes after the noun.
6. 'Eldest', 'elder', are used for persons, 'oldest', 'older' for inanimate objects.
7. 'Less' denotes degree, quantity; 'fewer' denotes number.

'Every' and 'each' can be used together correctly to convey very strong emphasis. Usually one of the two objectives is quite sufficient.
9. 'A few' means some. It is positive. 'Few' means nothing. 'A little' means something. 'Little' means nothing or nought.
10. 'Latter' means mentioned later in order.
11. 'Farther' is used for distance. 'Further' means additional.
12. There are some adjectives which are not used in comparative or superlative degrees such as 'supreme,' 'extreme', 'unique', 'preferable', 'right', 'square', 'round', 'unchangeable', 'universal', 'perfect', 'compete', 'golden', 'entire', 'ideal', 'eternal.
13. 'All' refers to number. 'Whole' refers to quantity.
14. 'Much', 'many', 'many a': 'Much' denotes quantity and 'many' denotes a number. 'Many a' means many times one thing. It is followed by a singular noun and takes a singular verb.
15. In the comparative degree use 'any other than'. In the superlative degree do not use 'any other than' but use 'the' before, and 'of all' after the superlative.
16. The 'er' sign of the comparative is not used when two qualities of the same thing or person are to be compared.
17. When two adjectives refer to the same subject and one of them is superlative, the other must also be superlative.
18. When 'both' is used as an adjective it should be followed by 'the'. With a possessive pronoun or noun, it should come before, and not after.
19. 'Only' is an adverb.
20. 'Rather' has force of the comparative. Double comparatives should not be used.
21. The comparative in 'er' is not used when we compare two qualities in the same person or thing. In that case we use 'more' before the adjective.

4

VERBS

INCORRECT	CORRECT
1. She was forced to *leave* her rights.	She was forced to *relinquish* her rights.
2. *Leave* the dog's leash.	*Let go* the dog's leash.
3. I *left* smoking long ago.	I *gave up* smoking long ago.
4. She has *left* dancing.	She has *given up* dancing.
5. If *I would have done that* course, I would have got this job.	If *I had done* that course, I *should* have got this job.
6. When *I shall visit* him, I shall bring up the subject.	When *I visit* him, I shall bring up the subject.
7. If he *resigned*, he will regret.	If he *resigns*, he will regret.
8. If *I shall* complain, I shall be wrong.	If *I* complain, I shall be wrong.
9. She *had been for walking* in the morning.	She *went for a walk* in the morning.
10. She said that she *saw* him last year.	She said that she *had seen* him last year.
11. She did not meet him because he *went out* before she arrived.	She did not meet him because he *had gone out* before she arrived.

	INCORRECT	CORRECT
12.	She began to cry before I *said* a word.	She began to cry before I *had said* a word.
13.	Yesterday I met a lady who *was* my teacher long ago.	Yesterday I met a lady who *had been* my teacher long ago.
14.	This cheating *was* going on *since* a long time.	This cheating *had been* going on *for* a long time.
15.	He asked *had I* booked his ticket.	He asked *if/whether/I had* booked his ticket.
16.	He *asked that* what are you doing.	He *asked what* we were doing.
17.	Sheila *asked can* she go home.	Sheila *asked if she* could go home.
18.	Radha *asked to Ravi* why he is late.	Radha *asked Ravi* why he was late.
19.	She does *not care for* what I say.	She *pays no attention* to what I say.
20.	He *does not care for* his health.	He *does not take care of* his health.
21.	She *does not care for* her work.	She *takes no care over* her work.
22.	I do not *care for what* you say.	I do not *care what* you say.
23.	No one *cared* for him after his mother died.	No *one took care* of him after his mother died.
24.	When I reached home I found that the guest *was* disappeared.	When I reached home I found that the guest *had* disappeared.
25.	Now, go home and *take* your food.	Now, go home and *have* your food.
26.	She *came to know* as to how he did this.	She *learnt* how he did this.
27.	He *came to know* why she was sad.	He *found out* why she was sad.
28.	She went to school to *know* music.	She went to school to *learn* music.

INCORRECT	CORRECT
29. Prema knows *to* swim.	Prema knows *how to* swim.
30. After a while, she *knew* her mistake.	After a while, she *realized* her mistake.
31. He was asked not to *cut* jokes in class.	He was asked not to *make* jokes in class.
32. He went out to *cut* his pencil.	He went out to *sharpen* his pencil.
33. The word is incorrect, *cut* it.	The word is incorrect, *scratch* it *out/erase* it.
34. Did they really *cut* his head?	Did they really *cut off* his head?
35. I *said to her* leave the room.	I *told her* to leave the room.
36. He *said to me* to go home.	He *told me* to go home.
37. He *asked* his servant to bring him some water.	He *told* his servant to bring him some water.
38. The servant *told* the master to let him go.	The servant *asked* the master to let him go.
39. The chairman *wanted that I should get* leave.	The chairman wanted *me to get* leave.
40. I want *that I should be* relieved.	I want *to be* relieved.
41. He is *troubling* his subordinates.	He is *ill-treating/oppressing* his subordinates.
42. He is *troubling* me.	He is *giving me trouble.* or He is *treating me badly.*
43. My neck is *paining*.	I *have pain* in my neck. or My neck is *hurting*.
44. His tooth is *paining*.	He has *a toothache*. or His tooth his *aching*.
45. I have *got hurt in* my leg.	I have *hurt* my leg.

INCORRECT	CORRECT
46. The principal *gave* a speech at the end of the function.	The principal *made* a speech at the end of the function.
47. I *put* my money in this box.	I *keep* my money in this box.
48. *Keep* this kettle on the table.	*Put* this kettle on the table.
49. He has just *given* his entrance examination.	He has just *sat for/taken* his entrance examination.
50. I *put up with* Kamal during my stay at Bombay.	Kamal *put me up* during my stay at Bombay.
51. I have disposed *off* my property.	I have disposed *of* my property.
52. We have *ordered for a* new car.	We have *ordered a* new car.
53. She has been finding it difficult *to pull on with* her work.	She has been finding it difficult *to manage* her work.
54. Can you *sit on a* bicycle?	Can you *ride a* bicycle?
55. When he saw me he *got down* from his bicycle.	When he saw me he *got off* his bicycle.
56. He *took out* his shoes before entering the room.	He *took off* his shoes before entering the room.
57. Please *see* my hand.	Please *look at* my hand.
58. She pleaded with him not to leave her but he would not *hear* me.	She pleaded with him not to leave her but he would not *listen* to her.
59. He had *put on* a cotton shirt yesterday.	He had *worn* a cotton shirt yesterday.
60. He came *putting* on a white cap.	He came *wearing* a white cap.
61. Roopa is *reading* in a convent school.	Roopa is *studying* in a convent school.
62. Peter *stood first* in his class.	Peter *was first* in his class.

INCORRECT	CORRECT
63. I invited her to my house but she *denied* to come.	I invited her to my house but *refused* to come.
64. People *respected* the President at the airport.	People *showed respect for* the president at the station.
65. When the principal accused me of misbehaviour I *had a mind* to speak out.	When the principal accused me of misbehaviour I had *intended* to speak out.
66. *It goes hard with him* to handle the situation at the factory.	*He finds it hard* to handle the situation at the factory.
67. In this situation we cannot *maintain our livelihood.*	In this situation we *cannot earn a living.*
68. He *struck a blow* on my face.	He *struck* me in the face. or He hit me in the face.
69. He *shot* the wild boar but missed.	He *shot at* the wild boar and missed.
70. I *went for* trekking and enjoyed.	I *went out* trekking and *enjoyed myself.*
71. Do not play mischiefs while I'm away.	Do not be up to mischief while I'm away.
72. After hitting an iceberg the ship *was drowned.*	After hitting an iceberg the ship *sank.*
73. Name the person who *invented* Greenland.	Name the person who *discovered* Greenland.
74. His timely action *prevented* him from harm.	His timely action *protected* him from harm.
75. We *lived* at the guest house for a day.	We *stayed* at the guest house for a day.
76. They were *filling water in their buckets.*	They were *filling their buckets with water.*
77. We easily *won* our opponents.	We easily *beat* our opponents.

INCORRECT	CORRECT
78. Ten minutes after the start we *made* our first goal.	Ten minutes after the start we *scored* our first goal.
79. The principal knew the boy *did* no fault.	The principal knew the *boy committed* no fault.
80. I'm busy *fairing out* my notes.	I'm busy *making a fair copy* of my notes.
81. We were *making* our drill when the accident took place.	We were *doing* our drill when the accident took place.
82. *Make* regular exercise, if you want to stay healthy.	*Take* regular exercise, if you want to stay healthy.
83. We hope he must come.	We hope he will come. or He must come.
84. The group is consisted of five men.	The group consists of five men.
85. Do you know who *found* the city of Delhi?	Do you know who *founded* the city of Delhi?
86. *Wish* him when he comes in.	*Greet* him when he comes in.
87. He was determined to *revenge* his sister.	He was determined to *avenge* his sister.
88. He *revenged* his enemies.	He *took revenge on* his enemies.
89. *It is written in this letter* that the incident did take place.	*The letter says* that the incident did take place.
90. He *thought* how she could have escaped.	He *wondered* how she could have escaped.
91. She had *marked* how he was operating.	She had *noticed* how he was operating.
92. You can *avail of this* opportunity to meet him.	You can avail *yourself of this* opportunity to meet him.
93. Kavita *is* absent for two weeks.	Kavita *has been* absent for two weeks.

INCORRECT	CORRECT
94. The crowd did nothing but *shouted*.	The crowd did nothing but *shout*.
95. Which city *you* like most?	Which city *do you* like most?
96. I do not like *you* coming late to office everyday.	I do not like *your* coming late to office everyday.
97. *Completing* the race, he collapsed.	*On completing* the race he collapsed.
98. *Being* a public holiday the shops were closed.	*It being* a public holiday the shops were closed.
99. *Shall* you help me in this project?	*Will* you help me in this project?
100. At the restaurant he *ordered for* a coke.	At the restaurant he *ordered* a coke.
101. Come what may, he *shall* take part in the race.	Come what may, he *will* take part in the race.
102. *Sitting* in the restaurant, he was attacked by the criminals.	*While he sat* in the restaurant, he was attacked by the criminals.
103. Praveen denied that *he had not met* the man.	Praveen denied that he *had met* the man.
104. Geeta *shall* answer my question.	Geeta *will* answer my question.
105. I *will* meet you in my office tomorrow.	I *shall* meet you in my office tomorrow.
106. The shopkeeper admitted that the man *has* given him the money.	The shopkeeper admitted that the man *had* given him the money.
107. Harish *pleased* at your proposal.	Harish is *pleased* at your proposal.
108. You are required to *give* a test in English.	You are required to *take* a test in English.

INCORRECT	CORRECT
109. Your teacher is preparing to *take* a test tomorrow.	Your teacher is preparing to *give* a test tomorrow.
110. Please *open* the tap.	Please *turn on* the tap.
111. She *closed* the tap.	She *turned off* the tap.
112. The principal with all the teachers *were* present.	The principal with all the teachers *was* present.
113. Every man, woman and child *were* out in the street.	Every man, woman and child *was* out in the street.
114. Namita as well as Kavita *are* intelligent.	Namita as well as Kavita *is* intelligent.
115. The committee *is* divided in *its* recommendation	The committee *are* divided in *their* recommendations.
116. I who *is* his father will pay for him.	I who *am* his father will pay for him.
117. You who *is* his friend should advise him.	You who *are* his friend should advise him.
118. Twenty kilometres *are* not a long distance.	Twenty kilometres *is* not a long distance.
119. One thousand rupees *are* a big sum.	One thousand rupees *is* a big sum.
120. No sooner he *received* the news than he left for home.	No sooner *did he receive* the news than he left for home.
121. Seldom he *visits* us.	Seldom *does he visit* us.
122. Not only *we shall* go to the beach but swim also.	Not only *shall we* go to the beach but swim also.
123. Neither he came nor she sent the book.	Neither did he come nor did he send the book.
124. Radio was *discovered* by Marconi.	Radio was *invented* by Marconi.
125. She *knows* to paint.	She *knows how* to paint.

INCORRECT	CORRECT
126. I *said to her* to come in.	I *told her* to come in.
127. Can you *see* these words in your dictionary for me?	Can you *look up* these words in your dictionary for me?
128. The notorious dacoit was finally *hung*.	The notorious dacoit was finally *hanged*.
129. He *tells* he is tried.	He *says* he is tired.
130. You shout at me as though as I *am* deaf.	You shout at me as if I *were* deaf.
131. People *seemed* to have known the use of fire in those days.	People *seem* to have known the use of fire in those days.

☞ NOTES

1. Intransitive verb cannot be used in the passive voice.
2. 'Say' is used to assert or declare; 'tell' to inform narrate, or command; `speak' to utter words; 'say' refers to the words, while 'speaking refers to the voice.
3. 'Hope' is your expectation with pleasure.
4. 'Will' with the first person denotes determination and 'shall' simple futurity.
5. Universal truths are always reported in the present tense.
6. After adjectives active, not passive, infinitive should be used.
7. 'As if' and 'as though' are always followed by a past conditional.
8. Words of quantity, like 'lots' and 'heaps', when used for a great number, require a singular verb unless they are followed by a plural noun. We say: 'There is lots of sugar', but 'lots of students were present'.
9. When the connective is 'as well as' the verb agrees in number and person with the first one.
10. 'Lest' is followed by a verb with 'should' as its auxiliary.
11. "Putting on clothes' refers to the act of dressing. Once the act is over, then the clothes are `worn'.
12. 'I shot the tiger' means that you hit and killed him.
13. Error is caused by two alternative idioms being combined.
14. 'Operate' in the surgical sense must only be used in the active voice.
15. Some verbs take reflexive pronouns after them. Other verbs are

'laid', 'dress', 'hide', 'spread', 'disperse', 'avail', etc. But these can be used without a reflexive pronoun also.
16. The sign of infinitive is not used after the verbs: 'need', 'make', 'bid', 'dare', 'feel', 'see', 'behold', 'hear', 'observe'.
17. The infinitive without 'to' is also used after 'rather than', would rather', 'had rather', 'had better, 'sooner than', etc.
18. Wrong relation of the participle with the noun.
19. The sequence of tenses: if the verb in the principal clause is in the past tense, the verb in the dependent clause should be in the past tense.
   (b) If the verb in the principal clause is in the present or future tense, the verb in the dependent clauses may be of any tense.
20. The present perfect tense is used in referring to a completed action.
21. When two nouns or pronouns are formed by 'not only' and 'but also', the verb must agree with the second noun or pronoun.
22. A verb should agree with its subject and not with the complement.
23. When two singular nouns express a single idea the verb is singular.
24. 'Many a' should always be followed by a singular noun and singular verb. But when 'many a' is followed by two nouns of distinct meanings the verb is plural, as: Many a boy and girl were playing
25. In certain words like 'bathe', 'break', 'dash', 'keep', 'more', 'open', 'draw', 'spread', 'sat', 'turn', 'feed', 'rest', 'hide', 'well', 'enlist', 'gather', 'burst', 'repent', 'qualify', 'make', 'form', 'stop', 'steel', 'lengthen', do not use reflexive pronouns such as 'himself', 'itself', 'herself', and 'myself'.
26. Verbs like 'avenge', 'absent', 'avail', 'acquit', 'drink', 'distinguish', 'resign', 'exert', 'overeat', 'enjoy', 'set', 'oversleep', 'overreach', 'apply' need a reflexive pronoun after them.
27. Verbs like 'regard', 'depict', 'represent', 'define', 'treat', 'mention', are followed by 'as'.
28. Verbs like 'call', 'appoint', 'elect', and 'think', are not followed by 'as'.
29. The noun or pronoun should be put in the possessive case.
30. The past perfect is generally used to show that a certain action or event took place before something else happened.
31. If there is one article or one thing, the verb is singular. If there are two articles or two things, the verb is plural.
32. When two singular nouns have the same idea, the verb is singular.
33. When a collective noun like 'crowd', 'fleet', 'committee', 'army', is thought as a whole acting together as one unit, it is used in the singular sense.

34. Some nouns like 'rest', 'variety', 'plenty', 'army', 'number', 'dozen', 'enemy', 'common', 'pair' are plural in meaning though they are singular in form, so the form of verb should be plural.
35. Two nouns connected by 'as well as', 'like', 'in addition to', 'besides', together', 'with' are followed by a verb in the singular, when the former of the two is in the singular.
36. Two or more singular nouns or pronouns connected by 'either ... or', 'neither ... nor', require a singular verb. If the subjects differ in number, or in person, the verb follows the number and person of the subject which stands nearest to it.
37. When 'either' or 'neither' are used as nouns or as adjectives, they must have a singular verb.
38. Two auxiliary verbs are used with one principal verb, when the form of the principal verb allows.
39. 'Every', 'each', 'everyone', 'either', 'neither', 'many a' are followed by a singular verb.
40. When adjectives like 'little', 'less', 'much', 'more', are used as nouns they must have a singular verb.
41. The verb comes before its subject when it is introduced by 'neither' or 'nor', even in case of 'no sooner', 'hardly', the verb comes before the subject.
42. In a subjective mood, when there is an expression of some wish or supposition, the verb is plural.
43. 'Will' and 'would' can be used in the sense of habit in all persons, present time being denoted by 'will' and the past time by 'would'.
44. The gerund with a preposition must be used instead of the infinite purpose.
45. We use a gerund and not an infinitive after the verbs 'persist', 'insist', 'stop', 'succeed', 'prevent', 'hinder'.
46. The gerund is a verbal noun like 'buying', 'going'. The verbs 'help', 'stop', 'avoid', 'dread', 'succeed', 'dislike', 'enjoy', 'remember', etc., take gerunds.
47. When a sentence beings with a participle, it qualifies the subject and should agree with a subject. Present participle is a verb ending in 'ing' - 'sitting', 'going', 'running'.
48. Some nouns like 'committee', 'council', 'cabinet', 'jury', 'crowd', 'majority' are singular or plural accordingly considered collectively or individually.
49. Use 'flow', 'flowed', 'fly', 'flew', 'flown' (for birds), 'flee', 'fled', 'fled'- (for persons).

'WILL', 'SHALL', 'WOULD', AND 'SHOULD'

INCORRECT	CORRECT
1. I *will* visit my parents next week.	I *shall* visit my parents next week.
2. I *will* be forty next year.	I *shall* be forty next year.
3. We *will* help him with his interview tomorrow.	We *shall* help him with his interview tomorrow.
4. You *will* join the school if you are successful in the interview.	You *shall* join the school if you are successful in the interview.
5. You *will* complete your work and then leave the classroom.	You *shall* complete your work and then leave the classroom.
6. You *will* make good the damage.	You *shall* make good the damage.
7. You *will* take on additional responsibilities.	You *shall* take on additional responsibilities.
8. She *will* take orders from me.	She *shall* take orders from me.
9. He *will* use my vehicle tomorrow.	He *shall* use my vehicle tomorrow.
10. They *will* apologize for the wrongs they have done.	They *shall* apologize for the wrongs they have done.
11. I *shall* come to see you tomorrow.	I *will* come to see you tomorrow.

INCORRECT	CORRECT
12. I *shall* dismiss if you continue to be disrespectful.	I *will* dismiss you if you continue to be disrespectful.
13. *Shall* he go with you?	*Will* he go with you?
14. *Will* I go with you?	*Shall* I go with you?
15. We *shall* attend your function.	We *will* attend your function.
16. We *shall* work over-time and complete the project.	We *will* work overtime and complete the project.
17. She *shall* return tomorrow.	She *will* return tomorrow.
18. *Shall* you be twenty-five next year?	*Will* you be twenty-five next year?
19. When I *shall* see her, I *shall* explain everything.	When I see her, I *shall* explain everything.
20. Until he *will* have owned up his crimes, he *will* be kept here.	Until he has owned up his crimes, he *will* be kept here.
21. Unless you check him Shyam *should* have his way.	Unless you check him, Shyam *would* have his way.
22. She *should* not agree to his proposal.	She *would* not agree to his proposal.
23. After dinner we *should*, normally, go for a walk.	After dinner we *would*, normally, go for a walk.
24. If I were there, I *will* have stopped him.	If I were there I *would* stop him.
25. He *should* ask you to reconsider you decision.	He *would* ask you to reconsider your decision.
26. If I *should* do wrong, she would be disappointed with me.	If I *did* wrong, she would be disappointed with me.

☞ NOTES

1. a) 'Shall' (with the subject in the first person) has a simple future meaning. 'I shall go'. 'Will' with the subject in the second and third persons has the same simple future meaning. 'You will see' means that a time is coming when you are going to see.

   b) 'Shall' with the subject in the second and third persons introduces the idea of compulsion.

   You shall (even if against your will).

   He shall obey (whether he likes it or not).

   c) 'Will' with the subject in the first person expresses determination.

   I will go (I am determined to go).

2. a) 'Should' with the first person and 'would' with the second and third persons are the correct auxiliaries of the conditional tense when there is no special force of meaning to be conveyed. They should be used as 'shall' and 'will' are used in the future tense. See I (a) above.

   b) 'Should' with the second and third persons means 'ought to. 'You should work hard'. (It is your duty to do so).

   c) 'Would' with the subject in the first person gives emphasis. 'We would like a holiday' (very much indeed). It also expresses determination although less definitely than in I (c) above. 'I would go if I got the chance' (though you doubt my words).

6

ADVERBS

INCORRECT	CORRECT
1. He *scarcely* sees us these days.	He *rarely* sees us these days.
2. She was *very kind enough* to offer me this job.	She was *so kind as* to offer me this job. or She was *kind enough* to offer me this job.
3. She got out of the difficult situation *anyhow*.	She got out of the situation *somehow*.
4. *To tell in brief* we are not prepared to take up this job.	*In short*, we are not prepared to take up this job.
5. I want to hear the story in *details*.	I want to hear the story in *detail*.
6. He travelled by a superfast train and reached Bombay *soon*.	He travelled by a superfast train and reached Bombay *quickly*.
7. He realises how much he has hurt you and is *very much* sorry.	He realises how much he has hurt you and is *very* sorry.
8. If she fails this time, she will be *nowhere*.	If she fails this time, she will be *ruined*.
9. She arrived *yesterday in the night*.	She arrived *last night*.

INCORRECT	CORRECT
10. We came to this city *before long*.	We came to this city *long ago*.
11. *Really speaking* we have excellent teachers.	*To speak the truth/As a matter of fact* we have excellent teachers.
12. Hardly *I have* had any sleep since I moved to the city.	Hardly *have* I had any sleep since I moved to the city.
13. Never *I have* seen such suffering in my life.	Never *have I* seen such suffering in my life.
14. She swims *much good* than I.	She swims *better* than I.
15. *What for* do you keep giving him money?	*Why* do you keep giving him money? or *What do you* keep giving him money *for*?
16. She sings *good*.	She sings *well*.
17. This job is *too* satisfying.	This job is *very* satisfying.
18. Accept his challenge; don't *behave cowardly*.	Accept his challenge; don't *behave in a cowardly* manner.
19. They live *miserly*.	They live in a *miserly way*.
20. *Just you had left* when I came.	*You had just left* when I came.
21. It was a good exhibition; I liked it *on the whole*.	It was a good exhibition; I liked *the whole of it*.
22. The situation was *very worse* than we had expected.	The situation was *much worse* than we had expected.
23. They left the room *by and by*.	They left the room *one by one*.
24. On seeing his child safe he was *very* relieved.	On seeing his child safe he was *much* relieved.
25. Calcutta is a *much* large city and a much dirty one too.	Calcutta is a *very* large city and a *very* dirty one too.

	INCORRECT	CORRECT
26.	The principal was *very* annoyed at her attitude.	The principal was *much* annoyed at her attitude.
27.	We found ourselves in a *much* amusing situation.	We found ourselves in a *very* amusing situation.
28.	He was *very* fast to be beaten.	He was *too* fast to be beaten.
29.	In this situation you should go *directly* to the principal.	In this situation you should go *direct* to the principal.
30.	He always behave *most* gentlemanly.	He always behaves in a *most* gentlemanly manner.
31.	Your decision may turn out to be *much* harmful than useful.	Your decision may turn out to be *more* harmful than useful.
32.	You reacted very *hasty*.	You reacted very *hastily*.
33.	Your language sounded *harshly*.	Your languages sounded *harsh*.
34.	Most *likely* the shops will remain closed tomorrow.	Most *probably* the shops will remain closed tomorrow.
35.	The *whole India* is proud at his achievement.	The *whole of India* is proud at his achievement.
36.	She did her sums *wrongly*.	She did her sums *wrong*.
37.	This bag is *very* heavy for me to carry.	This bag is *too* heavy for me to carry.
38.	This apple is *too* sweet.	This apple is *very* sweet.
39.	Call me anything else *than* an expert.	Call me anything *but* an expert.
40.	She was forced *to quickly* do her work.	She was forced *to do* her work *quickly*.
41.	He speaks the *truth always*.	He *always speaks* the truth.
42.	She *tells never* a lie.	She *never tells* a lie.
43.	She *comes* to my office *often*.	She *often comes* to my office.

	INCORRECT	CORRECT
44.	I feel *discouraged sometimes*.	I *sometimes feel discouraged*.
45.	This news is *very* good to be true.	This news is *too* good to be true.
46.	She was *quite* sorry to hear the sad news.	She was *very* sorry to hear the sad news.
47.	Does she sing well? *Of course,* she does.	Does she sing well? *Certainly,* she does.
48.	To be successful, *firstly* you should be regular, and *secondly* hard-working.	To be successful, *first* you should be regular, and secondly hard-working.
49.	I *never* remember having seen her.	I *do not* remember having seen her.
50.	He *eagerly wishes* to join his father.	He *wishes eagerly* to join his father.
51.	Finally, his mother *peacefully died*.	Finally, his mother *died peacefully*.
52.	We *explained briefly* our plans to the chairman.	We *briefly explained* our plans to the chairman.
53.	He *was fortunately* not present when the chairman came.	*Fortunately,* he was not present when the chairman came.
54.	The assailant was overpowered *at length*.	*At length* the assailant was overpowered.
55.	She is *enough intelligent* to know his real plan.	She is *intelligent enough* to know his real plans.
56.	*Sharmila* is somewhat short for her age.	*Sharmila* is rather short for her age.
57.	The police found her lying *senselessly*.	The police found her lying *senseless*.
58.	We have not seen him *long since*.	We have not seen him *for a long time*.

INCORRECT	CORRECT
59. He is *respected highly* in his country.	He is *highly respected* in his country.
60. He is *very* weak that he cannot walk.	He is *so* weak that he cannot walk.
61. He finished this work more *quick* than any of our staff.	He finished this work more *quickly* than any of our staff.
62. I shall be *very* obliged to you if you come.	I shall be *much* obliged if you come.
63. She left the country five years *before*.	She left the country five years *ago*.
64. Prema *wrote* me a week ago.	Prema *wrote to* me a week ago.
65. They have *invited* me *for* dinner.	They *invited* me *to* dinner.
66. Kavita *resembles to* her mother.	Kavita *resembles* her mother.
67. I've *discussed on* this subject with him.	I've *discussed this* subject with him.
68. Satya *recommended for me* to the principal.	Satya *recommended me* to the principal.
69. She begged pardon *from* the principal.	She begged pardon *of* the principal.
70. I *searched* the book everywhere.	I *searched for* the book everywhere.

☞ NOTES

1. a) 'Much' is used with adjectives or adverbs in the comparative degree; 'Very' is used with adjectives or adverbs in the positive degree.
   b) 'Much' is used with the past participles, 'very' is used with the present participles. But this rule is not always strictly followed.
   c) 'Very is used in the sense of 'really', 'truly'. As such it emphasises the adjectives in the superlative degree.

d) 'Very' is sometimes used and added to qualify 'much', as : 'This room is very much better than that'.
2. An adverb generally follows an intransitive verb and the objective of the transitive verb.
3. 'Since' is used for the point of time from which the action begins. 'For' is used for the period of time.
4. 'Of course' is used when the thing mentioned is naturally true.
5. 'As' is used after the verbs of description only such as 'mention', 'define', 'represent', 'portray', etc.
6. 'Too' is used where we imply some limit or correct standard. It denotes a kind of excess over the necessary limit or aim. When no limit or standard is implied, we use the adverb 'very' to qualify the adjective.
7. 'Ago' is used as an adverb of time. It is never used as a conjunction or preposition.
8. 'Else' should be followed by the adverb 'but' in the cases noted above.
9. The adverb 'enough' is generally used after the word modifies.
10. An adverb should not be used before an infinitive and its size.
11. Adjectives should not be used for adverbs.
12. The adverbs of time like 'ever', 'always', 'seldom', frequently', 'often', and 'sometimes', are generally used before the verbs they modify.
13. The adverb 'too' is used in the sense of more than enough but not in that of very much. 'To' is used also to mean also and as well; as, 'take the girls to the circus too.
14. Do not use 'quite' in the sense of 'very' or to a considerable degree.
15. 'Of course' is often loosely used for 'certainly'.
16. In an enumeration, say, 'firstly', 'secondly', and 'thirdly' use first which is an adverb.
17. As a rule, the word 'only' should be placed immediately before the word it is intended to modify.
18. With a transitive verb the adverb generally comes after the object. If, however, the object is long the adverb may come after the transitive verb : 'He writes carefully all the exercises he had to do'.
19. The use of 'never' for 'not' is incorrect, for 'never' means 'not ever' and not 'not'.
20. When the verb is intransitive, the adverb or the adverbial phrase is placed after the verb. But when the verb is transitive an adverb can be placed either before or after the verb.
21. An adverb should be placed at the beginning of a sentence when it

is intended to qualify not any word in particular, but the sentence as a whole.
22. Adjectives should not be used in place of adverbs.
23. 'Very' modifies adjectives or adverbs in a positive degree and much in the comparative degree.
24. Two negatives destroy each other.
25. 'So' as an adverb of degree must not be used absolutely without a correlative.
26. 'On the whole' is only used to sum up. Your opinion of something which is good or bad in parts.
27. 'After all' denotes in spite of what has gone before. It should not be used when we mean some natural consequence. 'Finally' will suit there better.
28. In colloquial speech the use of 'very' in such sentences passes as correct; as : 'I am very pleased', 'I am very tired', etc. But it is more correct to use 'much' in such cases.

PREPOSITIONS

INCORRECT	CORRECT
1. The principal congratulated me *for* my achievement.	The principal congratulated me *on* my achievement.
2. She wrote the letter *with* her blood.	She wrote the letter *in* her blood.
3. He slapped me *upon* the face.	He slapped me *on* the face.
4. There is no point *to go* to the station now.	There is no point *in going* to the station now.
5. He is an expert *to make* excuses.	He is expert *in making* excuses.
6. The boy has been complaining *for* toothache.	They boy has been complaining *of* toothache.
7. Everyone is anxious *for* your safety.	Everyone is anxious *about* your safety.
8. He left for Calutta *in* train.	He left for Calcutta *by* train.
9. You're answerable *for* the company for this loss.	You're answerable *to* the company for this loss.
10. I'm alive *for* consequences of my decision.	I'm alive *to the* consequences of my decision.
11. Did you meet Harish *upon* the way to your office?	Did you meet Harish *on* your way to the office?

45

INCORRECT	CORRECT
12. To save her child she jumped *in* the well.	To save her child she jumped *into* the well.
13. You'll have to answer *on* your misbehaviour.	You'll have to answer *for* your misbehaviour.
14. She has been acquitted *from* the charge of kidnapping.	She has been acquitted *of* the charge of kidnapping.
15. He caught me *at* the neck.	He caught me *by* the neck.
16. That cup is full *with* soup.	That cup is full *of* soup.
17. My brother is good *in* Mathematics.	My brother is good *at* Mathematics.
18. He did not agree *with* my proposal.	He did not agree *to* my proposal.
19. The workers decided to abide *with* the decision of the manager.	The workers decided to abide *by* the decision of the manager.
20. He has been accused *for* theft.	He has been accused *of* theft.
21. The administration was fully aware *about* the situation.	The administration was fully aware *of* the situation.
22. You must apologise *from* the teacher for your misbehaviour.	You must apologise *to* him for your misbehaviour.
23. The secretary assured the chairman *with* his honesty.	The secretary assured the chairman *of* his honesty.
24. You must attend *on* what has been decided at the meeting.	You must attend *to* what has been decided at the meeting.
25. I saw him absorbed *with* his studies.	I saw him absorbed *in* his studies.
26. The nurse is attending *to* your mother.	The nurse is attending *on* your mother.
27. The manager was angry *on* his staff.	The manager was angry *with* his staff.

INCORRECT	CORRECT
28. He was told to admit his wife *in* the hospital.	He was told to admit his wife *to* the hospital.
29. This city abounds *from* taxis.	This city abounds *in* taxis.
30. She is addicted *from* drugs.	She is addicted *to* drugs.
31. No one can deny her affection *to* her children.	No one can deny her affection *for* her children.
32. He will survive if he abstains *for* drugs.	He will survive if he abstains *from* drugs.
33. Now, you have no choice but to appeal *for* the Supreme Court.	Now, you have no choice but to appeal *to* the Supreme Court.
34. We have no access *with* the chairman	We have no access *to* the chairman.
35. He keeps believing *on* God.	He keeps believing *in* God.
36. You must avail *in* this opportunity.	You must avail *of* this opportunity.
37. The workers are bent *upon* destruction.	The workers are bent *on* destruction.
38. You must pay attention *on* what your father says.	You must pay attention *to* what your father says.
39. He has adapted himself *with* the new place.	He has adapted himself *to* the new place.
40. I'm not accustomed *for* this kind of music.	I'm not accustomed *to* this kind of music.
41. He is not very attached *with* his family.	He is not very attached *to* his family.
42. After much discussion they arrived *on* a conclusion.	After much discussion they arrived *at* a conclusion.
43. The principal was annoyed *on* us.	The principal was annoyed *with* us.

INCORRECT	CORRECT
44. Your company's terms are not acceptable *for* us.	Your company's terms are not acceptable *to* us.
45. There is no doubt the President will give his assent *on* the bill.	There is no doubt the President will give his assent *to* the bill.
46. The principal has acceded *with* our request.	The principal has acceded *to* our request.
47. God has bestowed his blessings *upon* us.	God has bestowed his blessings *on* us.
48. She seems to have lost the confidence *from* her partner.	She seems to have lost the confidence *of* her partner.
49. This place is crowded; beware *from* pickpockets.	This place is crowded; beware *of* pickpockets.
50. You must behave respectfully *with* your elders.	You must behave respectfully *towards* your elders.
51. I have just made a complaint *for* you to the principal.	I have just made a complaint *against* you to the principal.
52. I'll speak to the boss on behalf *for* you.	I'll speak to the principal on behalf *of* you.
53. They have been blessed *of* a son.	They have been blessed *with* a son.
54. The ill-fated train was bound *to* New Delhi.	The ill-fated train was bound *for* New Delhi.
55. Whenever I come I see you busy *in* your work.	Whenever I come I see you busy *with* your work.
56. He is known to boast *for* his estate.	He is known to boast *of* his estate.
57. I never thought he would back out *from* his word.	I never thought he would back out *of* his word.
58. He begged pardon *from* his teacher.	He begged pardon *of* his teacher.

INCORRECT	CORRECT
59. It is better for you to comply *to* your parent's wishes.	It is better for you to comply *with* your parent's wishes.
60. Your friend is capable *for* doing anything.	Your friend is capable *of* doing anything.
61. He has been made conscious *with* his shortcomings.	He has been made conscious *of* his shortcomings.
62. He is contented *to* his life as a tailor.	He is contented *with* his life as a tailor.
63. The accident took place when the bus collided *to* a truck.	The accident took place when the bus collided *with* a truck.
64. You can always count *for* our help.	You can always count *on* our help.
65. I'm happy to see you cured *from* all your diseases.	I'm happy to see you cured *of* all your diseases.
66. We have contributed some money *for* the building fund.	We have contributed some money *towards* the building fund.
67. Do you compare life *with* a cricket match?	Do you compare life *to* a cricket match?
68. You must take care *for* your health.	You must take care *of* your health.
69. She has been charged *of* murder.	She has been charged *with* murder.
70. Over a hundred people have died *from* cholera in the city.	Over a hundred people have died *of* cholera in the city.
71. The book fair will commence *from* the eighth of February.	The book fair will commence *on* the eighth of February.
72. I devote two hours *for* my exercises daily.	I devote two hours *to* my exercises daily.
73. Did you call *on* my house?	Did you call *at* my house?

INCORRECT	CORRECT
74. This place is devoid *from* any order.	This place is devoid *of* any order.
75. The businessman called *at* his client yesterday.	The businessman called *on* his client yesterday.
76. The robbers deprived us *from* all our belongings.	The robbers deprived us *of* all our belongings.
77. My friend deals *with* textiles.	My friend deals *in* textiles.
78. Mother Teresa's life is dedicated *for* the service of the destitutes.	Mother Teresa's life is dedicated *to* the service of the destitutes.
79. I am desirous *for* publishing a book.	I am desirous *of* publishing a book.
80. I owe my life *for* the driver who averted a fatal accident.	I owe my life *to* the driver who averted a fatal accident.
81. My approach to this problem is different *with* yours.	My approach to this problem is different *from* yours.
82. Emergency has been imposed *in* that country.	Emergency has been imposed *on* that country.
83. She died *of* exhaustion.	She died *from* exhaustion.
84. Ignorance *from* law is no excuse.	Ignorance *of* law is no excuse.
85. I have dissuaded him *of* buying that property.	I have dissuaded him *from* buying that property.
86. The old lady is hard *from* hearing.	The old lady is hard *of* hearing.
87. I've deposited all my money *in* the State Bank.	I deposited all my money *with* the State Bank.
88. This is the same girl I told *you*.	This is the same girl I told *you about*.
89. I don't like to see you *hanker* with money.	I don't like to see you hanker *after* money.

INCORRECT	CORRECT
90. He was envious *from* his wife's success.	He was envious *of* his wife's success.
91. You are not entitled *for* this allowance.	You are not entitled *to* this allowance.
92. Are you not familiar *to* her antics?	Are you not familiar *with* her antics?
93. I find him fit *to* join work now.	I find him fit *for* joining work now.
94. He has full faith *with* his secretary.	He has full faith *in* his secretary.
95. I prefer unemployment *than* work here.	I prefer unemployment *to* work here.
96. Her house is infested *of* insects.	Her house is infested *with* insects.
97. My principal is pleased *at* my teaching.	My principal is pleased *with* my teaching.
98. Please introduce me *with* your friend.	Please introduce me *to* your friend.
99. He was not happy to part *from* all his possessions.	He was not happy to part *with* all his possessions.
100. She has very intimate relations *to* Praveen.	She has very intimate relations *with* Praveen.
101. Everyone was moved *with* tears at his sad story.	Everyone was moved *to* tears at his sad story.
102. Our product is superior *from* theirs.	Our product is superior *to* theirs.
103. His lust *to* wealth finally drove him to his death.	His lust *for* wealth finally drove him to his death.
104. You must not jeer *on* others.	You must not jeer *at* others.
105. There seems to be no limit *on* her craving for luxuries.	There seems to be no limit *to* her craving for luxuries.

INCORRECT	CORRECT
106. No one is jealous *on* your success.	No one is jealous *of* your success.
107. He has never been loyal *with* his company.	He has never been loyal *to* his company.
108. Did you knock *on* my door?	Did you knock *at* my door?
109. Please remind me *about* my appointment.	Please remind me *of* my appointment.
110. We presented him an expensive watch.	We presented him *with* an expensive watch.
111. The matter has now been referred *for* the chairman for decision.	The matter has now been referred *to* the chairman for decision.
112. She prevailed *on* him to give up business.	She prevailed *upon* him to give up business.
113. I do not wish to reason everybody on this matter.	I do not wish to reason *with* everybody on this matter.
114. Nobody has prohibited him *to* leave the country.	Nobody has prohibited him *from* leaving the country.
115. He has no prejudice *for* those belonging to other states.	He has no prejudice *against* those belonging to other states.
116. The workers protested *for* the arrest of their leader.	The workers protested *against* the arrest of their leader.
117. Are you fully prepared *to* your interview?	Are you fully prepared *for* your interview?
118. Everyone is proud *on* your achievements.	Everyone is proud *of* your achievements.
119. The principal is accused of being partial *for* some teachers.	The principal is accused of being partial *to* some teachers.
120. It is nice to know your views are identical *to* mine.	It is nice to know your views are identical *with* mine.

INCORRECT	CORRECT
121. You must remember me *with* your sister.	You must remember me *to* your sister.
122. Stduents are clamouring *to* more freedom.	Students are clamouring *for* more freedom.
123. You must stand *with* me in times of trials.	You must stand *by* me in times of trials.
124. You are absolved *from* all the charges.	You are absolved *of* all the charges.
125. Are you averse *for* ladies travelling with you?	Are you averse *to* ladies travelling with you?
126. Our college is affiliated *with* your university.	Our college is affiliated *to* your university.
127. So early in life, he is afflicted *from* diabetes.	So early in life he is afflicted *with* diabetes.
128. I enjoy complete control *on* my department.	I enjoy complete control *over* my department.
129. We are not amenable *for* any kind of external pressure.	We are not amenable *to* any kind of external pressure.
130. I saw the girl jump *in* the well.	I saw the girl jump *into* the well.
131. You must stop meddling *with* the affairs of the company.	You must stop meddling *in* the affairs of the company.
132. The old man divided his wealth *between* his five children.	The old man divided his wealth *among* his five children.
133. She is overwhelmed *in* grief at the loss of her son.	She is overwhelmed *with* grief at the loss of her son.
134. The boys are playing cricket *from* morning.	The boys are playing cricket *since* morning.
135. They live in Sholapur *at* Maharashtra.	They live *at* Sholapur *in* Maharashtra.

INCORRECT	CORRECT
136. The judge divided the property *among* the two claimants.	The judge divided the property *between* the two claimants.
137. The farmers were compensated *about* the loss of their property.	The farmers were compensated *for* the loss of their property.
138. We started living here *since* 30th April 1993.	We started living here *from* 30th April 1993.
139. Are you disappointed *on* the offer of such a post?	Are you disappointed *with* the offer of such a post?
140. Will you pour some water *in* my glass?	Will you pour some water *into* my glass?
141. *In* my way to office I see a lot of beggars.	*On* my way to office I see a lot of beggars.
142. The children have gone *in* the playground.	The children have gone *to* the playground.
143. I want a piece of paper to write.	I want a piece of paper to write *on*.
144. I saw some boys sitting *upon* the bench.	I saw some boys sitting *on* the bench.
145. Our house is very spacious to live.	Our house is very spacious to live *in*.
146. I saw a frog spring *on* his shoulder.	I saw a frog spring *upon* his shoulder.
147. He used the gun to shoot.	He used the gun to shoot *with*.
148. The oldman stopped the intruder *by* his hand.	The old man stopped the intruder *with* his hand.
149. Please don't compare Nelson Mandela *to* Mother Teresa.	Please don't compare Nelson Mandela *with* Mother Teresa.
150. He entered *into* the room through the back door.	He entered the room through the back door.

INCORRECT	CORRECT
151. You reached *at* the airport too late.	You reached the airport too late.
152. We have entered *in* an agreement with your company.	We have entered *into* an agreement with your company.
153. You have copied my article word *by* word.	You have copied my article word *for* word.
154. The beggar is blind *from* one eye.	The beggar is blind *of* one eye.
155. She is confident *to get* this job.	She is confident *of getting* this job.
156. These days he abstains drinks.	These days he abstains *from* drinks.
157. A person in your position should *refrain* to make public statements.	A person in your position should *refrain from* making public statements.
158. Under your leadership we are deprived *from* some of our freedom.	Under your leadership we are deprived *of* some of our freedom.
159. The present director is successful *to control* corruption.	The present director is successful *in controlling* corruption.
160. We were not invited *for* dinner.	We were not invited *to* dinner.
161. Could you kindly send the letter *on* my new address?	Could you kindly send the letter *to* my new address?
162. She is fortunate to be married *with* you.	She is fortunate to be married *to* you.
163. Nobody prevented you *to go* to college.	Nobody prevented you *from going* to college.
164. I have *dispensed* the services of my driver.	I have *dispensed with* the services of my driver.
165. Our house is situated *besides* the post office.	Our house is situated *beside* the post office.

INCORRECT	CORRECT
166. I will always remain grateful *for* you.	I will always remain grateful *to* you.
167. This is the same girl I spoke to *you*.	This is the same girl I spoke to *you about*.
168. *He is ill since* four months.	*He has been ill for* months.
169. This is my first time to play football *since* a long time.	This is my first game of football *for* a long time.
170. My umbrella is different *to* yours.	My umbrella is different *from* yours.
171. Your face *resembles* to hers.	Your face *resembles* hers.
172. Our captain is faster *than* you in attack.	Our captain is faster *to* you in attack.
173. You should *pray God everyday*.	You should *pray to God* everyday.
174. He *wrote me* from New York.	He *wrote to me* from New York.
175. You *explain him* your position.	You *explain to him* your position.
176. The festival of Diwali corresponds *with* Christmas.	The festival of Diwali corresponds *to* Christmas.
177. He *suggested me* a different course of action.	He *suggested to me* a different course of action.
178. Whatever his compulsions at home, he *goes on* his work.	Whatever his compulsion at home, he *goes to* his work.
179. I'm obliged *of you* for this favour.	I'm obliged *to you* for this favour.
180. She *is favourite* with her colleagues.	She *is a favourite* with her colleagues
181. She *told to him* not to harass her.	She *told him* not to harass her.

INCORRECT	CORRECT
182. We did not ask any question *to her*.	We did not *ask her* any question.
183. Alok did best *from* our group.	Alok did best *in* our group.
184. My course begins *from* September 15th.	My course begins *on* September 15th.
185. The doctor says, Ben will be cured *from* his headaches.	The doctor says, Ben will be cured *of* his headaches.
186. There are many advantages *from working* part-time.	The advantages *of working* part-time are many.
187. There is a saying *in* the Christians that if anyone strikes you on cheek, you must show him the other.	There is a saying *among* the Christians that if anyone strikes you on one cheek, you must show him the other.
188. Don't you think we've wasted much time *in* details?	Don't you think we've wasted much time *over* (on) details?
189. He comes to school riding *in* a bicycle.	He comes to school riding *on* a bicycle.
190. There is no harm *to sit* in the sun.	There is no harm *in sitting* in the sun.
191. When you take down such important notes, it is better to write *with* ink.	When you take down such important notes, it is better to write *in* ink.
192. He is fortunate to be riding *on* a car to office.	He is fortunate to be riding *in* a car to office.
193. I was surprised to see him sitting *on* a tree.	I was surprised to see him sitting *in* a tree.
194. If you want to get there quickly, this is the road *to go*.	If you want to get there quickly, this is the road *to go by*.
195. She offered me a chair *to sit*.	She offered me a chair to sit *on*.
196. Vehicles are called *with* different names.	Vehicles are called *by* different names.

	INCORRECT	CORRECT
197.	I accompanied *with my* friends to Simla.	I accompanied *my* friends to Simla.
198.	She spends too much money *for* luxuries.	She spends too much money *on* luxuries.
199.	He has gone to Bombay *to do* some business.	He has gone to Bombay *on* business.
200.	After he returned from work he went *for riding*.	After he returned from work he went riding/for a ride.
201.	The members of the staff *discussed on* the matter in detail.	The members of the staff *discussed* the matter in detail.
202.	When the purse was *searched* it was found.	When the purse was *searched for* it was found.
203.	When I helped him, he was pleased *on* me.	When I helped him, he was pleased *with* me.
204.	When his father handed him over to the police she *pitied on* him.	When his father handed him over to the police she *pitied* him.
205.	Aren't you pleased *on* me?	Aren't you pleased *with* me?
206.	Our company showed remarkable progress *during* 1991-1994.	Our company showed remarkable progress *between 1991 and 1994*.
207.	There was peace in the country *between* Ashoka's reign.	There was peace in the country *during* Ashoka's reign.
208.	After the annual sports meet, we *asked a holiday*.	After the annual sports meet, we *asked for a holiday*.
209.	We met *with the chairman* yesterday.	We *met the chairman* yesterday.
210.	This wall is built *by* bricks.	This wall is built *of* bricks.
211.	He was absent *due to* illness.	He was absent *owing to* illness.

	INCORRECT	CORRECT
212.	You should immediately inform *him our mistake*.	You should immediately inform *him of our mistake*.
213.	Looking for her, I went to the *back side* of her house.	Looking for her, I went to the *back of (behind)* her house.
214.	He comes to the office *by* foot.	He comes to the office *on* foot.
215.	Nobody prevented her *to come*.	Nobody prevented her *from coming*.
216.	Our office will *compensate* the loss.	Our office will *compensate for* the loss.
217.	The match was *between* Tamil Nadu *against* Karnataka.	The match was *between* Tamil Nadu and Karnataka.
218.	I strongly *object your* remarks.	I strongly *object to your* remarks.
219.	We are not blind *of* his misdeeds.	We are not blind *to* his misdeeds.
220.	You must *attend your* work immediately.	You must *attend to your* work immediately.
221.	Are you angry *at* me ?	Are you angry *with me*?
222.	I do not *desire for a change* just now.	I do not *desire a change* just now.
223.	He has been suffering *with* fever.	He has been suffering *from* fever.
224.	He has been kind *upon* me.	He has been kind *to me*.
225.	The principal has *called for a meeting*.	The principal has *called a meeting*.
226.	Who is satisfied *by* her work?	Who is satisfied *with* her work?
227.	The chairman signed *on the* agreement.	The chairman signed *the* agreement.

INCORRECT	CORRECT
228. After much discussion we've arrived *to* this conclusion.	After much discussion we've arrived *at* this conclusion.
229. You must *knock the* door before entering my room.	You must *knock at the* door before entering my room.
230. He has been repeatedly finding fault *in* her work.	He has been repeatedly finding fault *with* her work.
231. What is the time *on* your watch?	What is the time *by* your watch?
232. I'm translating this story *in* English.	I'm translating this story *into* English.
233. She is jealous *with* me.	She is jealous *of* me.
234. You seem to be accustomed *with* hot weather.	You seem to be accustomed *to* cold weather.
235. He set *fire to his* house.	He set *his house on fire*.
236. Will you *listen me* for a while?	Will you *listen to me* for a while?
237. I admire your taste *in* painting.	I admire your taste *for* painting.
238. She told all that she had found out *on* his face.	She told all that she had found out *to* his face.
239. She has something *to ask from you*.	She has something *to ask you*.
240. We are indifferent *about* Hindi films.	We are indifferent to *Hindi* films.
241. Leave the food *upon* the table.	Leave the food *on* the table.
242. Wash your hands *in* water.	Wash your hands *with* water.
243. He has been operated *for* cataract.	He has been operated *upon* for cataract.
244. When she heard the shocking news she burst *with* tears.	When she heard the shocking news she burst *into* tears.

INCORRECT	CORRECT
245. She has been aspiring *for* that post.	She has been aspiring *to* that post.
246. Your name *precedes before* mine in the list.	Your name *precedes mine* in the list.
247. I intend contributing something *for* this fund.	I intend contributing something *to* this fund.
248. He has no prejudice *for* her.	He has no prejudice *against* her.
249. You have complained *of* me of my parents.	You have complained *against* me to my parents.
250. He is suspected *for* stealing the purse.	He is suspected *of* stealing the purse.
251. When they arrived I was working *on* my desk.	When they arrived I was working *at* my desk.
252. All of us are surprised *by* his failure.	All of us are surprised *at* his failure.
253. Here are the notes that you *asked*.	Here are the notes that you *asked for*.
254. We drove *till* the end of the road.	We drove *to* the end of the road.
255. I waited *up to* 8 o'clock.	I waited *till* 8 o'clock.
256. When he saw you he *got down from* his bicycle.	When he saw you he *got off* his bicycle.
257. Are you *keen to go* abroad?	Are you *keen on going* abroad?
258. These sandals will *wear off* soon.	These sandals will *wear out* soon.

☞ **NOTES**

1. 'After' is used with a period of past time and not with a period of future time.
2. 'Till' is used for time and 'to' is used for place.
3. 'On' is used in speaking of things at rest and 'upon' of things which are in motion.

4. 'In' and 'at' are used in speaking of things which are at rest or fixed and 'to' and 'into' in speaking of things which are in motion, viz. 'she is in bed.' 'She ran to college.' 'The rat went into the trap.'
5. 'Meditate', when referring to the past, takes a preposition but not when referring to the future.
6. 'Between' and 'among': 'Between' is used for two things and 'among' for more than two.

'In' and 'within' : 'In' means after the lapse of the appointed time, 'within' means before the end of it (appointed time).

'At' and 'in' : when these prepositions are used to denote time space, 'at' refers to a small extent, and 'in' to a wider, a larger one.

'Into' and 'in' : signifies motion or rest in a place, 'into' shows motion from one place to another.

'With' and 'by' : 'With' denotes the instrument with which a thing is done, and 'by' denotes the agent or the doer.

CONJUNCTIONS

INCORRECT	CORRECT
1. Both Shikha and her mother *were not present*.	Neither Shikha nor her mother *was present*.
2. As he has to attend a meeting *so* he won't be seeing you.	As he has to attend a meeting he won't be seeing you.
3. I will admit *no* other man but Praveen.	I will admit *no* other man *than* Praveen.
4. She has no other claim *except* her good looks.	She has no other claim *than* her good looks.
5. He talks *like* his brother.	He talks *as* his brother *does*.
6. She is *not only* beautiful *but* intelligent.	She is not only beautiful *but also* intelligent.
7. She *not only* lost her friend but also her job.	She lost *not only* her friend, her job also.
8. *Both* Sunil *as well as* Ravi are selected to play.	*Both* Sunil and Ravi are selected to play.
9. Elephants are *both found* in Asia and Africa.	Elephants are *found both* in Asia and in Africa.
10. She is very generous *but* helps the needy.	She is very generous *and* helps the needy.
11. City life is tense *and* village life is relaxed.	City life is tense *but* village life is relaxed.

	INCORRECT	CORRECT
12.	He won't sing *before* he is compelled.	He won't sing *unless* he is compelled.
13.	Neither did I speak *nor he spoke*.	Neither did I speak *nor did he*.
14.	I doubt *that* she will meet him.	I doubt *whether* she will meet him.
15.	The choice is between a decent job *or* unlimited money.	The choice is between a decent job *and* unlimited money.
16.	His feat was *not heroic* as it is made out to be.	His feat was *not as heroic* as it is made out to be.
17.	His secretary is *equally* capable as mine.	His secretary is *as* capable as mine.
18.	Before she *will come* you will have left.	Before *she comes* you will have left.
19.	*Because* he is insincere *therefore* no one gives him a job.	He is insincere; *therefore* no one gives him a job.
20.	She took a different stance *than* what she used to take.	She took a different stance *from* what she used to take.
21.	*When* you ignored her she went away.	*Since* you ignored her she went away.
22.	I fear she might run away.	I fear *that* she might run away.
23.	I hope you'll get well soon.	I hope *that* you'll get well soon.
24.	I will look after her *until* she is with me.	I will look after her *as long as* she is with me.
25.	Now you have come, you relieve me.	Now *that* you have come, you relieve me.
26.	*As he comes* I shall go.	*As soon as he comes*, I shall go.
27.	I had scarcely reached the airport *than* the flight took off.	I had scarcely reached the airport *when* the flight took off.

INCORRECT	CORRECT
28. I had no choice *than* to sell the house.	I had no choice *but* to sell the house.
29. *Immediately* she saw me she recognised me.	*As soon as* she saw me she recognised me.
30. Isn't he *equally good* as his father?	Isn't he *as good as* his father?
31. She was unfriendly, *therefore* I went away.	She was unfriendly, *so* I ran away.
32. She is *not* beautiful *or* intelligent.	She is *neither* beautiful *nor* intelligent.
33. When he saw the boss *then* he was nervous.	When he saw the boss, he was nervous.
34. I shall try *and* find him at the fair.	I shall try *to* find him at the fair.
35. He was worried *as soon as* I returned.	He was worried *until* I returned.
36. *Not only he is* the cook but the owner of the restaurant.	*Not only is he* the cook but he is also the owner of the restaurant.
37. That is the *reason* he does not meet anyone in public.	That is the *reason why* he does not meet anyone in public.
38. Though she worked hard *but* she failed.	Though she worked hard *yet* she failed.
39. No sooner I reached the office *when* it began to rain.	No sooner did I reach the office *than* it began to rain.
40. She is the same lady *whom* you met last night.	She is the same lady *that* you met last night.
41. She is *good*, if not better than Shalini.	She is *as good as*, if not better than, Shalini.
42. I regard him my saviour.	I regard him *as* my saviour.
43. Tom will be appointed to the head coach.	Tom will be appointed the head coach.

INCORRECT	CORRECT
44. He commands as if he *is* the boss.	He commands as if he *were* the boss.
45. You act as though you *are* the owner of the place.	You act as though you *were* the owner of the place.
46. Answer intelligently lest you *may not be* rejected.	Answer intelligently *lest* you should be rejected.
47. I left the place lest you all *should* be *not* caught.	I left the place lest you all *should* be caught.
48. Unless you *do not* meet him you will not convince him of your innocence.	Unless you *meet* him you will not convince him of your innocence.
49. You must wait here *until I do not come.*	You must wait here *until I come.*
50. I *have bought* this house two weeks since.	I *bought* this house two weeks since.
51. *I did not see* you since you met with an accident.	*I have not seen* you since you met with an accident.
52. She asked me *that how you are.*	She asked me *how I was.*
53. He asked me *that where* his brother was.	He asked me *where* his brother was.
54. *Either* your action was right or wrong.	Your action was *either* right *or* wrong.
55. She *or* he was hasty.	*Either* she *or* he was hasty.
56. *Neither* he is rich *nor* intelligent.	He is *neither* rich *nor* intelligent.
57. I have *never* seen him or heard of him.	I have *neither* seen him *nor* heard of him.
58. He did not buy it *nor* borrow it.	He did not buy it *or* borrow it.

INCORRECT	CORRECT
59. Did you go to your house or office?	Did you go to your house or *to your* office?
60. Do not go *until* I come back.	Do not go *till* I come back.
61. I have *got* nothing to add.	I *have* nothing to add.
62. He doesn't know me *like* you do.	He doesn't know me *as* you do.
63. Wait *while* I come, I won't be long.	Wait *till* I come, I won't be long.
64. So far I am concerned you are selected.	So far *as* I am concerned you are selected.
65. They did nothing else *than* shout.	They did nothing else *but* shout.
66. His work is incomplete. *Therefore,* his case cannot be taken up.	His work is incomplete. His case, *therefore,* cannot be taken up.
67. The boss asked him *that whether* he knew what he was talking about.	The boss asked him *whether* he knew what he was talking about.
68. I enquired *that where* your office was.	I enquired *where* your office was.
69. You must wait here *until* it rains.	You must wait here *while* it rains.
70. I prefer to be without job *than* be a slave.	I prefer to be without job *rather than* be a slave.
71. Could you, please, tell me *when is the next bus?*	Could you, please, tell me *when the next bus is?*
72. Tell me when *are you* coming back.	Tell me when *you are* coming back.
73. *Until* you work hard, you will succeed.	*As long as* you work hard you will succeed.

INCORRECT	CORRECT
74. He must *either* leave or I.	*Either* he *or* I must leave.
75. *Supposing if* your father returns now, what will you do?	Supposing *(or if)* your father returns now, what will you do?
76. *Though* she is frail *but (yet, still)* she runs fast.	*Though* she is frail, she runs fast.
77. *As he is* ill *so* he cannot play.	*As he is* ill, he cannot play.
78. He travels by bus. *Because* he cannot afford a scooter.	He travels by bus *because* he cannot afford a scooter.
79. Because he is the cleverest, *therefore (so)*, he tops the class.	Because he is the cleverest, he tops the class.
80. *As I opened* the door *at that time* I heard the gun-shot.	*As I opened* the door, I heard the gun-shot.
81. *If* he is clever *then* he will score good marks.	If he is clever, he will score good marks.
82. She is the cleverest student in the class *and* she failed.	She is the cleverest student in the class *but* she failed.
83. Did he call you *as a fool*?	Did he call you *a fool*?
84. Until he makes a confession, he must be interrogated.	He must be interrogated until he makes a confession.
85. Not only *she will go*, but *also she will* stay there.	Not only *will she go, but she will also* stay there.
86. I have bought many classics *as* "The Treasure Island" *and etc.*	I have bought many classics *such as* "The Treasure Island"
87. I am fond of all foods *as for an example* ice-cream.	I am fond of all foods, *for example,* ice-cream.
88. I want to know *as to why* she has been delayed.	I want to know *why* she has been delayed.
89. Everyone is glad *for* tomorrow is a holiday.	I am glad *because* tomorrow is a holiday.

	INCORRECT	CORRECT
90.	You were busy *therefore* I went away.	You were busy *so* I went away.
91.	She was trying to concentrate, *at that time* you were disturbing her.	While she was trying to concentrate you were disturbing her.
92.	That is an expensive pen, you are writing with it.	That is an expensive *pen with which* you are writing.
93.	This is my cousin, I have spoken to you about him.	This is my cousin *about whom* I have spoken to you.

☞ NOTES

1. After the adjective 'others' use 'than'. Don't use from, except, but.
2. 'As' is not followed by 'so' except for the sake of emphasis : 'As you sow, so shall you reap.'
3. 'Both' has a positive sense. In the negative sense, we should use 'neither/ nor' in the place of 'both'.
4. If the conjunction 'both' is used, it should be followed by 'and' and not by 'as well as'. Also 'both' should be placed immediately before the words to which it refers.
5. 'And' is to join two words or clauses of the same nature. 'But' is to join two antithetical clauses.
6. The proper correlative of 'not only' is 'but' or 'but also'. They should be followed by words of the same parts of speech.
7. 'Like' should not be used as a conjunction in the sense of 'as', although such a use may be allowed in conversation.
8. 'Neither' is always complemented by 'nor'. 'Neither' is followed by an auxiliary verb, 'nor' should be followed by the same auxiliary verb.
9. 'Come' should be taken not to use 'that' in place of 'if', 'when', 'whether', and 'though'.
10. 'Equally' and 'as' are not true correlatives. When 'as' is used as a conjunction to denote equality of degree, it should be preceded by 'as' in the affirmative clause or by 'so' or 'as' in a negative one.
11. When the conjunctions 'when', 'while', 'tell', 'before', and 'after' are used in the subordinate sentences with reference to some future event, they are not followed by a verb in the future tense even when the verb in the principal clause is in the future.

12. 'Because' and 'therefore' should not be used in the same sentence.
13. After 'different' do not use 'than', use 'from'.
14. 'When' refers to a point of time. It should not be used for 'since'.
15. Use 'that' after 'fear' and 'hope'.
16. 'Hardly' is followed by 'when' and 'scarcely' by 'before' or 'when', but not by 'but', 'than', or 'that'.
17. 'Though' is followed by 'yet', and not by 'but'.
18. 'No sooner' is followed by 'than', not by 'then' or 'when' or 'but'.
19. Certain words such as 'mention', 'treat', 'depict', 'define', 'regard', 'portray', 'present', 'describe', are always followed by 'as'.
20. Certain words (verbs) such as 'make', 'call', 'elect', 'appoint', 'choose', 'name', 'think', 'consider', are not followed by 'as' or 'to be'.
21. Do not use the present tense after 'as if' and 'as though'; use 'were' in the present tense and 'had been' in the past tense.
22. 'Lest' is negative and should not be followed by 'not'. After 'lest' use 'should.'
23. 'Unless', 'until', 'so that', 'if not', should not be used in a negative sentence.
24. 'That' should not be used before a sentence in the direct narration, or after a verb denoting a question in the indirect speech.
25. 'Therefore' is used after a word or phrase that is emphasised.
26. In a subordinate clause, the question form is changed to the assertive form.
27. Words thought of together must be kept together :
    a) A relative pronoun or verb should be placed as close to its antecedent as possible.
    b) When a noun or a noun phrase or a clause is in opposition to a noun, it should not be separated from it by any word.
    c) An adverb qualifying a sentence as a whole is placed at the beginning.

SEQUENCE OF TENSES

INCORRECT	CORRECT
1. Arthur *could win* this match if he tries.	Arthur *could win* this match if he *tried*.
2. Mamta *said* that she will wait for me.	Mamta *said* that she *would wait* for me.
3. She *enquired* if the robber *is* caught.	She *enquired* if the robber *was* caught.
4. Ravi *made* a request that I *shall accompany* him.	Ravi *made* a request that I *should accompany* him.
5. The boss *wanted to know* why I *am* late.	The boss *wanted to know* why I *was* late.
6. She told me that he *was* addicted to drugs.	She told me that he *is* addicted to drugs.
7. His secretary disclosed that he *was* always punctual.	His secretary disclosed that he *is* always punctual.
8. You could borrow this book if you *like*.	You could borrow this book if you *liked*.
9. Her father wanted to know how she *has* done in her examinations.	Her father wanted to know how she *had* done in her examinations.
10. I know that the earth *went* round the sun.	I know that the earth *goes* round the sun.

INCORRECT	CORRECT
11. The doctor *asked* the mother if the child has already been vaccinated.	The doctor *asked* the mother if the child *had* already been vaccinated.
12. He is very upset because he *is* punished by his father.	He is very upset because he *was* punished by his father.
13. The principal said that honesty *was* the best policy.	The principal said that honesty *is* the best policy.
14. The preacher said that God *was* merciful.	The preacher said that God *is* merciful.
15. My colleague hinted that he *wants* to resign.	My colleague hinted that he *wanted* to resign.
16. He studies daily for four hours lest he *will* fail again.	He studies daily for four hours lest he *should* fail again.
17. She talks as though she *is* the only actress in the country.	She talks as though she *were* the only actress in the country.
18. She walks carefully lest she *falls*.	She walks carefully lest she *should fall*.
19. He orders us about, as if he *is* the boss.	He orders us about, as if he *were* the boss.
20. She works diligently lest *will* lose her job.	She works diligently lest she *should* lose her job.
21. The girl screamed as if she *was* beaten.	The girl screamed as if she *were* beaten.
22. Euclid proved that the three angles of a triangle *were* equal to two right angles.	Euclid proved that the three angles of a triangle *are* equal to two right angles.
23. We found out that he *is* guilty.	We found out that he *was* guilty.
24. The manager replied that he *will come* soon.	The manager replied that he *would come* soon.

	INCORRECT	CORRECT
25.	Newton discovered that the force of gravitation *made* apples fall to the ground.	Newton discovered that the force of gravitation *makes* apples fall to the ground.
26.	I never thought I *will* walk again.	I never thought I *would* walk again.
27.	I *am doing* my tests last week when my sister came to visit me.	I *was doing* my tests last week when my sister came to visit me.
28.	After completing my high school I *apply* to study there.	*After completing* my high school I *applied* to study there.
29.	I *will listen* to some good music when I *finished* my work.	I *will listen* to some good music when I *finish* my work.
30.	It *rains* everyday for the past one week.	It *rained* everyday for the past one week.
31.	My father was *having a nap* when the phone *was ringing*.	My father *was having a nap* when the phone *rang*.
32.	He fell down and hurt himself *while he played* cricket.	He fell down and hurt himself *while playing* cricket.
33.	Have you finished reading the book I *lend* you last week.	Have you finished reading the book I *lent* you last week?
34.	When we were having supper last night, my brother *tells* the parents of his intention to give up college.	When we were having supper last night, my brother *told* the parents of his intention to give up college.
35.	He likes it here, but the hot weather *is bothering* him.	He likes it here, but the hot weather *bothers* him.
36.	Not many people *listen* to plays on the radio these days.	Not many people *listened* to plays on the radio these days.
37.	I *cook*, dear. Go and answer the doorbell.	I *am cooking*, dear, Go and answer the doorbell.

INCORRECT	CORRECT
38. The next time I find you wasting time, I *dismiss* you.	The next time I find you wasting time *I'll dismiss* you.
39. I am disappointed because my best friend *fail* in the examination.	I am disappointed because my best friend *has failed* in the examination.
40. I *am* cleaning up the place, when she came home.	I *was* cleaning up the place when she came home.
41. When I got back from work, the children *played* blissfully.	When I got back from work, the children *were playing* blissfully.
42. Grandfather *sleeps*. Please, do not disturb him.	Grandfather *is sleeping*. Please do not disturb him.
43. In August, it rains very often and this *caused* floods.	In August, it rains very often and this *causes* floods.

ARTICLES

INCORRECT	CORRECT
1. *The rice* is a summer crop.	*Rice* is a summer crop.
2. I met *strange man* in the park.	I met *a strange man* in the park.
3. *The beggars* are waiting at the gate.	*Beggars* are waiting at the gate.
4. *Elephants* of Africa have large ears.	*The elephants* of Africa have large ears.
5. Prakash is *sincere* boy.	Prakash is *a sincere* boy.
6. The people of our city have elected him *the mayor*.	The people of our city have elected him *mayor*.
7. My parents want me to join *the government* service.	My parents want me to join *government service*.
8. The main is *social animal*.	Man is *a social animal*.
9. *The children* like to play.	*Children* like to play.
10. In Calcutta we stayed *at hotel*.	In Calcutta we stayed *at a hotel*.
11. This is *famous* movement.	This is *a famous* movement.
12. *Water* of most Indian rivers is polluted.	*The water* of most Indian rivers is polluted.
13. *India of today* is progressive.	*The India of today* is progressive.

	INCORRECT	CORRECT
14.	The beggar wants nothing less than *one-rupee coin*.	The beggar wants nothing less than *a one-rupee coin*.
15.	You may give him *hundred rupees* just now.	You may give him *a hundred rupees* just now.
16.	*Wisdom* of our ancient sages is to be admired.	*The wisdom* of our ancient sages is to be admired.
17.	*President* of our country is on a trip abroad.	*The President* of our country is on a trip abroad.
18.	Shivaji was *famous* ruler of Marathas.	Shivaji was *a famous* ruler of *the* Marathas.
19.	*Apple* is my favourite fruit.	*The apple* is my favourite fruit.
20.	Calcutta is *most* populous city in India.	Calcutta is *the most* populous city in India.
21.	Archie is *cleverer* of the two brothers.	Archie is *the cleverer* of the two brothers.
22.	*Ramayana* is popular all over the world.	*The Ramayana* is popular all over the world.
23.	*Guilty* must be punished.	*The guilty* must be punished.
24.	*Himalayas* are the highest mountains in the world.	*The Himalayas* are the highest mountains in the world.
25.	He grabbed me by *my* collar.	He grabbed me by *the* collar.
26.	*Gangetic Plain* is one of the most fertile regions of the world.	*The Gangetic Plain* is one of the most fertile regions of the world.
27.	Everyone wants *Indian Ocean* to be declared a zone of peace.	Everyone wants *the Indian Ocean* to be declared a zone of peace.
28.	He buys cars *by dozens*.	He buys cars by *the* dozens.
29.	*Nile* is one of the longest rivers of the world.	*The Nile* is one of the longest rivers of the world.

INCORRECT	CORRECT
30. *The both* brothers are good hockey players.	*Both the* brothers are good hockey players.
31. What you say is *a news* to me.	What you say is *news* to me.
32. Cotton is grown extensively in *Deccan*.	Cotton is grown extensively in *the Deccan*.
33. Who was *president* of India soon after Independence?	Who was *the president* of India soon after Independence?
34. You may go to sleep; I will not make *noise*.	You may go to sleep; I will not make *a noise*.
35. I was *first* to reach the office today.	I was *the* first to reach the office today.
36. She is known to be a good artist and *a sculptor*.	She is known to be a good artist and *sculptor*.
37. I know how fine *singer* she is!	I know how fine *a singer* she is!
38. Isn't *pen* mightier than sword?	Isn't *the pen* mightier than the sword?
39. *Bus* arrived early today.	*The bus* arrived early today.
40. She had visited us *previous* day.	She visited us *the previous* day.
41. His secretary leads him by *nose*.	His secretary leads him by *the nose*.
42. Before leaving for school she had drunk *the water*.	Before leaving for school she had drunk *water*.
43. He died of *the diabetes*.	He died of *diabetes*.
44. I am in trouble; please lend me *few* rupees.	I am in trouble; please lend me *a few* rupees.
45. You may drink *water* kept on the table.	You may drink *the water* kept on the table.
46. *Recent* happenings in the country were distressing.	*The recent* happenings in the country were distressing.

INCORRECT	CORRECT
47. He has resigned from his post. What *fool* he is!	He has resigned from his post. What *a fool* he is!
48. *Educated* Indians are truly concerned about the population explosion.	*The educated* Indians are truly concerned about the population explosion.
49. He is a good man and *an accomplished* officer.	He is *a* good and *accomplished* officer.
50. The President, Prime Minister and *Chief Justice* are meeting today.	The President, the Prime Minister, and *the Chief Justice* are meeting today.
51. We are at *a* historical place.	We are at *an* historical place.
52. If you want *employment,* you must work hard.	If you want *an employment,* you must work hard.
53. Take *a umbrella* with you.	Take *an umbrella* with you.
54. You are *honest* businessman.	You are *an honest* businessman.
55. *An European* must have made such a statement.	*A European* must have made such a statement.
56. You must be *a M.A.* in English.	You must be *an M.A.* in English.
57. He is *a M.L.A.* from our constituency.	He is *an M.L.A.* from our constituency.
58. You proposal requires *an early* attention.	Your proposal requires *early* attention.
59. I saw her about *a* hour ago.	I saw her about *an* hour ago.
60. UNICEF is *international* organisation.	*The* UNICEF is *an international* organisation.
61. The author, *artist* and *doctor* met at my place.	*The* author, *the* artist and *the* doctor met at my place.
62. The Bible, *Koran* and *Gita* have the same importance in my life.	*The* Bible, *the* Koran, and *the* Gita have the same importance in my life.

	INCORRECT	CORRECT
63.	The sun, *moon* and *stars* are heavenly bodies.	*The* sun, *the* moon and *the* stars are heavenly bodies.
64.	This is *quite* revolutionary recommendation.	This is *quite a* revolutionary recommendation.
65.	Those who are not *the members* of the club cannot play golf here.	Those who are not *members* of the club, cannot play golf here.
66.	The majority of people living in this colony belong to *Hindu Community*.	The majority of *the* people living in this colony belong to *the Hindu Community*.
67.	*One thing* that I like about this place is its cleanliness.	*The one thing* that I like about this place is its cleanliness.
68.	Goa is known as *Rome* of the East.	Goa is known as *the Rome* of the East.
69.	Kalidas is *Shakespeare* of India.	Kalidas is *the Shakespeare* of India.
70.	*The running* waters were the cleanest.	*Running* waters were the cleanest.
71.	I have purchased this car from *the Ashok Motors*.	I have purchased this car from Ashok Motors.
72.	*The people* must look after the security of their neighbourhood.	*People* must look after the security of their neighbourhood.
73.	*People of Japan* are very industrious.	*The people of Japan* are very industrious.
74.	*The honesty* is the best policy.	*Honesty* is the best policy.
75.	*Love of wealth* drove him to his doom.	*The love of wealth* drove him to his doom.
76.	*Truth* of your statement can be challenged.	*The truth* of your statement can be challenged.
77.	The children leave *the school* at 1.30 p.m.	The children leave *school* at 1.30 p.m.

INCORRECT	CORRECT
78. I did not *shake the hands* with her.	I did not *shake hands* with her.
79. Decorations are *out of the place* here.	Decorations are *out of place* here.
80. He looked at her from *the head to the foot*.	He looked at her *from head to foot*.
81. His mischief came to *the light* when I opened the box.	His mischief came to *light* when I opened the box.
82. We walked through the busy marketplace *hand in the hand*.	We walked through the busy marketplace *hand in hand*.
83. She has removed the bed, *the table* and *the chairs* from her room.	She has removed the bed, *table* and *chairs* from her room.
84. I heard *noise* coming from the next room.	I heard *a noise* coming from the next room.
85. Please, don't disturb her, she has *headache*.	Please, don't disturb her, she has *a headache*.
86. It is *quarter* to four now.	It is *a quarter* to four now.
87. They decided to stay in the hills for *few* days more.	They decided to stay in the hills for *a few* days more.
88. *Camel* is known as ship of the desert.	*The* camel is known as *the ship* of the desert.
89. He has scored high marks in *the Geography*.	He has scored high marks *in Geography*.
90. Didn't you know that cloth is sold *by metre*?	Didn't you know that cloth is sold *by the metre*?
91. Why are you in such *great hurry*?	Why are you in such *a great hurry*?
92. My sister is *great singer* and dancer.	My sister is *a great singer* and dancer.

INCORRECT	CORRECT
93. He is *the* student of Presidency College.	He is *a* student of Presidency College.
94. They want *an* university for their state.	They want *a* university for their state.
95. We don't have *an* union in our organisation.	We don't have *a* union in our organisation.
96. He is *an* useful person to have around.	He is *a* useful person to have around.
97. I felt that it was *an* one-sided match.	I felt that it was *a* one-sided match.
98. There was *an* hole in the wall.	There was *a* hole in the wall.
99. It is *a* honour for me to be dining with you.	It is *an* honour for me to be dining with you.
100. He is *Kapil Dev* as far as fast bowling goes.	He is *a Kapil Dev* as far as fast bowling goes.
101. *Car* you are looking for is not produced anymore.	*The car* you are looking for is not produced anymore.
102. *Sooner* you meet him, *better* it is.	*The sooner* you meet him, *the better* it is.
103. She is *a girl* we are looking for.	She is *the girl* we are looking for.
104. When he read that poem *poet in him* was troubled.	When he read that poem *the poet in him* was troubled.
105. They left the city *at the daybreak*.	They left the city at *daybreak*.
106. He was quite fine *at the breakfast*.	He was quite fine *at breakfast*.
107. He is determined to achieve his goal by *the fair* or *the foul* means.	He is determined to achieve his goal by *fair* or *foul* means.

INCORRECT	CORRECT
108. He arrived here *on the horseback*.	He arrived here *on horseback*.
109. Please, don't *lose the heart*, things will improve.	Please, don't *lose heart*, things will improve.
110. At dawn, we *set the sail*.	At daybreak we *set sail*.
111. At *the dead of night* the attack began.	At *dead of night* the attack began.
112. He has succeeded *by the dint of* hard work.	He has succeeded *by dint of* hard work.
113. The news reached us by *the word of mouth*.	The news reached us by *word of mouth*.
114. Nobody advised him to *leave the school*.	Nobody advised him to *leave school*.
115. He stood up and we *followed the suit*.	He stood up and we *followed suit*.

☞ NOTES

1. When two adjectives refer to one person the verb is singular and the article is not repeated.
2. In case of different persons the articles should be repeated.
3. a) The definite article 'the' is placed before nouns which cannot be applied to more than one object, e.g., 'the moon', 'the world', 'the sun', 'the Gita', 'the Bible', 'the poles', 'the north', 'the Vedas', etc.
   b) It is placed before an adjective to show it as a whole class, e.g., 'the wise', 'the rich', 'the learned'.
   c) It is placed before the names of nations, e.g., 'the Indians', 'the Chinese'.
   d) It is used before the names of rivers, e.g., 'the Ganges', 'the Sutlej', before the names of the groups of islands, e.g., 'the West Indies', 'the Andamans', before the names of gulfs or oceans. e.g., the 'Indian Ocean', 'the Arabian gulf'; before the ranges of mountains, e.g, 'the Alps', before the descriptive names of the countries or provinces, e.g., 'the Punjab', 'the Deccan'.
   e) The definite article is omitted before abstract nouns, material nouns, and collective nouns, except in certain cases where some

noun is used in restricted and specialised forms, e.g., 'the love of money', 'the people of India', 'the gold of America'.
4. The articles are omitted in many phrases made by transitive verb, followed by their objects, when the verbs and the objects cannot be considered as separate entities.
5. The articles are omitted in prepositional phrases.
6. When different objects are numbered, the articles are omitted for brevity and emphasis.
7. 'A' is used before a word beginning with a consonant sound, e.g., 'a cow', 'a man', 'a dog', 'a fan'.
8. 'A' is used before any word beginning with the 'u' sound pronounced as 'u'-(yoo), e.g., 'a European', 'a union', 'a university', 'a useful pen'. But when 'u' is not pronounced as 'yoo', it is preceded by the 'u' article 'an', e.g., an urge', 'an uncle'.
'A' is also used before 'o' pronounced as 'wa', e.g., 'a one-eyed man', 'a one-rupee note', 'a one-sided argument'.
'A' is again used before a word beginning with an aspirated 'h', e.g., 'a hole', 'a house'; use 'an' in place of 'a' where 'h' is silent, e.g., 'an honest man', 'an hour', 'an honour', 'an heir'.
9. 'An' is used:
   a) Before a vowel, e.g., 'an inkpot', 'an umbrella', 'an enemy', 'an owl', 'an orange'.
   b) Before a word beginning with a silent 'h', e.g., 'an honest man', 'an hour', 'an heir'.
   c) Before a consonant, with sounds like a vowel, e.g., 'an M.B.B.S.', 'an M.A.', 'an L.L.B.', 'an S.P.'.
10. We use 'a' or 'an' when a proper noun is used in the sense of a common noun, e.g., 'Gandhi is a Socrates of India.', 'Kalidas is a Shakespeare of India.'
11. 'A' is used before a common noun in the singular word to single out an individual, e.g., the representation of a class.
12. 'The' is used before the names of seas, mountains, rivers, lakes, oceans, names of seasons, natural phenomenon, direction, holy books, newspapers, buildings, provinces, group of islands, the moon, the sun, the earth, the sky, the games, the north, the public, the world, the universe.
'The' is used before denoting a nationality or a community, e.g., 'the Indians', 'the English'. 'The' is used before descriptive use of some countries or states, e.g., 'the United States of America', 'the Deccan', 'the Punjab'.
13. 'The' is used when a singular noun is meant to represent a whole class.

14. 'The' is used when we speak of a particular person, a thing or one already referred to or known to the speaker.
15. 'The' is used with the superlatives because they specify singular objects.
16. We use 'the' as an adverb with a comparative, e.g., 'the merrier', 'the more'.
17. 'The' is used before nouns employed in a special sense.
18. 'The' is used in fixed idiomatic phrases, e.g., 'put to the test', 'in the wrong', 'in the dark', 'to the rescue', 'on the contrary'.
19. 'The' is not used before the following:
    a) Before proper nouns, unless they are used as common nouns, e.g., 'Kalidas', 'Bombay'.
    b) Before abstract nouns, e.g., 'truth', 'beauty', 'honesty'.
    c) Before names of materials, e.g., 'gold', 'silver', 'copper'.
    d) Before plural nouns that denote a class, e.g., 'Poets love nature'.
    e) Before names of diseases, sports, sciences, things single in kind, e.g., 'God', 'dancing', 'hockey', 'medicine', 'heaven', 'cricket', 'plague', 'cholera'.
    f) Before the nouns in certain idiomatic phrases, e.g., 'At a daybreak', 'to bring wood', 'take to 'heart', 'at breakfast', 'catch fire', 'by name', 'by air', 'by sea', 'in debt', 'by fair or foul means', 'on horseback', 'to lose heart', 'to set foot', 'to give ear', 'to set sail', 'ingest', 'to take offence', 'to take out', 'by leaps and bounds', 'out of reach', 'at dead of night', 'to shake hands', 'by dint of', 'by word of mouth', 'to follow suit', 'to leave school', 'to take oath', 'to call in mind', 'to live from hand to mouth', 'out of place'.
    g) Before days of the week, seasons, time of the year, e.g., 'Sunday', 'Deepawali', 'June'. Collective nouns used in a general sense do not take the definite article, e.g., 'Parliament', 'society', 'cattle', 'manking', 'posterity'.
    h) Before names of regular meals, names of things single in kind, e.g., 'dinner', 'lunch', 'breakfast', 'hell', 'god', 'heaven'.
    i) Before certain titles and names indicating relationship, e.g., 'Emperor Ashoka', 'President Nasser', 'Raj Bahadur'.
    j) Before a noun used in its widest sense, e.g., 'Man is mortal', 'What kind of flower is it ?'
    k) Before plural nouns used to denote a class in a general sense, e.g.,'Lawyers are generally clever'.

11

SINGULAR AND PLURAL NUMBERS

INCORRECT	CORRECT
1. Are these *mangos* from your trees?	Are these *mangoes* from your trees?
2. *Momentos* were distributed to all the participants.	*Momentoes* were distributed to all the participants.
3. Tell me more about *volcanos*.	Tell me more about *volcanoes*.
4. You will not find wild *buffalos* in this region.	You will not find wild *buffaloes* in this region.
5. Old *pianos* are not easy to come by these days.	Old *pianoes* are not easy to come by these days.
6. Have you seen *bamboos* growing there?	Have you seen *bambooes* growing there?
7. They served rare *dishs* at the dinner.	They served rare *dishes* at the dinner.
8. All our *branchs* have been informed of the latest changes.	All our *branches* have been informed of the latest changes.
9. Many *lifes* were lost in the earthquake.	Many *lives* were lost in the earthquake.
10. We have ordered new *saves* for the office.	We have ordered new *safes* for the office.

	INCORRECT	CORRECT
11.	Both the *chieves* have been informed of the meeting.	Both the *chiefs* have been informed of the meeting.
12.	Are there still *serves* in some countries ?	Are there still *serfs* in some countries ?
13.	The seven *dwarves* were kind to Snow White.	The seven *dwarfs* were kind to Snow White.
14.	I am still to see the *prooves* of my articles.	I am still to see the *proofs* of my articles.
15.	The *thiefs* had covered their tracks well.	The *thieves* had covered their tracks well.
16.	All the *wifes* were also invited to the function.	All the *wives* were also invited to the function.
17.	Wash your *foots* before you come in.	Wash your *feet* before you come in.
18.	Did you brush your *tooths* this morning?	Did you brush your *teeth* this morning?
19.	*Mouses* have caused havoc in this house.	*Mice* have caused havoc in this house.
20.	There is an effective medicine to get rid of *louses*.	There is an effective medicine to get rid of *lice*.
21.	He uses all his *oxes* to plough the fields.	He uses all his *oxen* to plough the fields.
22.	She is worried about her *childs*.	She is worried about her *children*.
23.	How many *sheeps* did you see in the meadow?	How many *sheep* did you see in the meadow?
24.	*Deers* do not live here anymore.	*Deer* do not live here anymore.
25.	We bought six *dozens* pears from the vendor.	We bought six *dozen* pears from the vendor.
26.	This car cost me four *lakhs* rupees.	This car cost me four *lakh* rupees.

INCORRECT	CORRECT
27. At the weighing-in the boxer weighed twenty *stones*.	At the weighing-in the boxer weighed twenty *stone*.
28. He wore new *trouser* for the party.	He wore new *trousers* for the party.
29. May I borrow your *scissor*?	May I borrow your *scissors*?
30. Grandfather forgot where he left his *spectacle*.	Grandfather forgot where he left his *spectacles*.
31. Please convey our *thank* to your mother.	Please convey our *thanks* to your mother.
32. He makes sure that alms *is* given to every beggar.	He makes sure that alms *are* given to every beggar.
33. Mathematics *are* taught in every school today.	Mathematics *is* taught in every school today.
34. Politics *are* not a favourite with me.	Politics *is* not a favourite with me.
35. The news he has brought *are* not good.	The news he has brought *is* not good.
36. The cattle *is* roaming the streets in our city.	The cattle *are* roaming the streets in our city.
37. The *cattles* are in the field.	The *cattle* are in the field.
38. We won the match by an *inning* and five runs.	We won the match by an *innings* and five runs.
39. Whose poultry *is* this?	Whose poultry *are* these?
40. The *peoples* are fed up with this government.	The *people* are fed up with this government.
41. The many *people* of the world have different customs.	The many *peoples* of the world have different customs.
42. The gentry of the town *was* present to welcome the president.	The gentry of the town *were* present to welcome the president.

INCORRECT	CORRECT
43. Both their *son-in-laws* came to visit them.	Both their *sons-in-law* came to visit them.
44. They are my *steps-sister*.	They are my *stepsisters*.
45. The three *commander-in chiefs* are invited to the function.	The three *commanders-in-chief* are invited to the function.
46. The *maids-servant* of the neighbourhood gather in the park every evening.	The *maid-servants* of the neighbourhood gather in the park every evening.
47. He is good to his *man-servants*.	He is good to his *men-servants*.
48. The *passer-bys* stopped and laughed at him.	The *passers-by* stopped and laughed at him.
49. Add two *spoonsful* of sugar to my coffee.	Add two *spoonfuls* of sugar to my coffee.
50. She gave two *handsfuls* of rice to him.	She gave two *handfuls* of rice to him.
51. He has two brothers and two *sisters*.	He has two *brothers* and *sisters*.
52. All the men and women in this community are my *brothers*.	All the men and women in this community are my *brethren*.
53. I saw a lot of *fishes* in the pool.	I saw a lot of *fish* in the pool.
54. This is a country of *genie*.	This is a country of *geniuses*.
55. Pay my *respect* to your parents.	Pay my *respects* to your parents.
56. Were you playing with *dies?*	Were you playing with *dice*?
57. *Physic* is my favourite subject.	*Physics* is my favourite subject.
58. The criminal was put in *fetter*.	The criminal was put in *fetters*.
59. Indian *force* is being sent on a peace-keeping mission.	Indian *forces* are being sent on a peace-keeping mission.
60. He purchased two pairs of *shoe*.	He purchased two pairs of *shoes*.

INCORRECT	CORRECT
61. I don t like his *hanger-ons*.	I don't like his *hangers-on*.
62. I am enchanted by *these sceneries*.	I am enchanted by *this scenery*.
63. Two *lords-justices* were present in the court.	Two *lord-justices* were present in the court.
64. I did not take the *appendixes* seriously.	I did not take the *appendices* seriously.
65. The boy was taking the *swines* for grazing.	The boy was taking the *swine* for grazing.
66. Thank you for the *informations* you sent.	Thank you for the *information* you sent.
67. Your book does not include the English *alphabets*.	Your book does not include the English *alphabet*.
68. I still remember the *poetries* I learnt as a child.	I still remember the *poetry* I learnt as a child.
69. Did you buy your *furnitures* recently?	Did you buy your *furniture* recently?
70. I have never seen a *three-feet* ruler.	I have never seen a *three-foot* ruler.
71. You may not have to use your *forces* against her.	You may not have to use your *force* against her.
72. Everyone recognizes him as a man of *letter*.	Everyone recognizes him as a man of *letters*.
73. I am not too fond of *vegetable*.	I am not too fond of *vegetables*.
74. The *poors* gather at his gate every morning.	The *poor* gather at his gate every morning.
75. She is true to her *words*.	She is true to her *word*.
76. He is sixty but his *hairs are* not grey.	He is sixty but his *hair is* not grey.
77. He has two grey *hair*.	He has two grey *hairs*.

GENDER

INCORRECT	CORRECT
1. His *male dog* looks smaller than his *female dog*.	His *dog* looks smaller than his *bitch*.
2. The *earless* is out of town.	The *countess* is out of town.
3. The cow did not see the *male cow* approaching.	The cow did not see the *bull (ox)* approaching.
4. The *buckess* was shot while the buck escaped.	The *doe* was shot while the buck escaped.
5. She is a *bachelor;* she lives alone.	She is a *spinster;* she lives alone.
6. The wife of the chief minister is the *patron* of our club.	The wife of the chief minister is the *patroness* of our club.
7. He has married a *Jew*.	He has married a *Jewess*.
8. All the gentlemen and *women* rose to their feet as the President entered the hall.	All the gentlemen and *the ladies* rose to their feet as the President entered the hall.
9. The woman was a *giant* compared with the others.	The woman was a *giantess* compared with the others.
10. She came riding on a *female horse*.	She came riding on a *mare*.

INCORRECT	CORRECT
11. Monks and *monkesses* have arrived in large numbers.	Monks and *nuns* have arrived in large numbers.
12. We do not keep the *female ducks* with *male ducks*.	We do not keep the *ducks* with the *drakes*.
13. She is the *manager* in her father's firm.	She is the *manageress* in her father's firm.
14. This temple has a *woman priest*.	This temple has a *priestess*.
15. She is the only living *czar* in Russia now.	She is the only living *czarina* in Russia now.
16. The *female lion* kept a close watch on her brood.	The *lioness* kept a close watch on her brood.
17. What do you see in the field, a peacock or a *female peacock*?	What do you see in the field, a peacock or a *peahen*?
18. The *male sparrow* helped the *female sparrow* build the nest.	The *cock-sparrow* helped the *hen-sparrow* build the nest.
19. How many *male* and *female actors* are present on the stage?	How many *actors* and *actresses* are present on the stage?
20. Victoria was a popular *emperor*.	Victoria was a popular *empress*.
21. Have you seen the duke and the *dukess* recently?	Have you seen the duke and the *duchess* recently?
22. She is the *administrator* here.	She is the *administratrix* here.
23. She claims to be our *landlord*.	She claims to be our *landlady*.
24. We are without milk today because the *milk-woman* did not come.	We are without milk today because the *milkmaid* did not come.
25. I knew it was a *male bee* sitting on the flower.	I knew it was a *drone* sitting on the flower.
26. She is my *brother's daughter*.	She is my *niece*.

PROVERBS

INCORRECT	CORRECT
1. Absence makes *heart* grow fonder.	Absence makes *the heart* grow fonder.
2. When *cat's* away, mice will play.	When *the cat's* away, *the* mice will play.
3. Out of *the sight,* out of *the* mind.	Out of *sight,* out of mind.
4. *The lightning* never strikes twice in the same place.	*Lightning* never strikes twice in the same place.
5. When angry, count *hundred.*	When angry count *a hundred.*
6. Don't count *the chickens* before they are hatched.	Don't count *your chickens* before they are hatched.
7. He laughs *the best* who laughs *the* last.	He laughs *best* who laughs last.
8. *Appearance is* deceptive.	*Appearances are* deceptive.
9. *Everything* that glitters is not gold.	*All* that glitters is not gold.
10. All clouds *do not bring* rain.	All clouds *bring not* rain.
11. Better *ask* the way than go astray.	Better *to ask* the way than go astray.

INCORRECT	CORRECT
12. Better *rule* than be ruled by the rout.	Better *to rule* than be ruled by the rout.
13. If you wish to know *the man* give him *the authority*.	If you wish to know *a man* give him *authority*.
14. Every man cannot be *the master*.	Every man cannot be *a master*.
15. Give *the thief* enough rope and he'll hang himself.	Give *a thief* enough rope and he'll hang himself.
16. Two blacks do not make *one white*.	Two blacks do not make *a white*.
17. Faith will move *the mountains*.	Faith will move *mountains*
18. Speak *only* when you are spoken to.	*Speak* when you are spoken to.
19. Do not *throw* your pearls before the swine.	Do not *cast* your pearls before swine.
20. Variety is *spice* of life.	Variety is *the spice* of life.
21. Don't change *the/your horses* in midstream.	Don't change *horses* in midstream.
22. *Rolling stone* gathers no moss.	*A rolling stone* gathers no moss.
23. One cannot put *the clock back*.	One cannot put *back the clock*.
24. You cannot make *the crab* walk straight.	You cannot make *a crab* walk straight.
25. *Man* is known by the company he keeps.	*A man* is known by the company he keeps.
26. When in Rome, do as *Romans* do.	When in Rome, do as *the* Romans do.
27. *A rotten apple* injures its neighbours.	*The rotten apple* injures its neighbours.
28. Poverty is *mother* of crime.	Poverty is *the* mother of crime.

INCORRECT	CORRECT
29. *Pot* calls kettle black.	*The* pot calls *the* kettle black.
30. If the cap *fits you,* wear it.	If the cap *fits,* wear it.
31. If you play with *the fire, you'll* get burnt.	If you play with *fire,* you get burnt.
32. All *the men* are mortal.	All *men* are mortal.
33. Nothing is *as* certain as death.	Nothing is *so* certain as death.
34. He that is once born *must* die.	He that is once born, *once must* die.
35. Death defies *doctor.*	Death defies *the* doctor.
36. Death keeps *not the* calendar.	Death keeps *no* calendar.
37. *Good people* die young.	*The good* die young.
38. *Good life* makes good death.	*A good life* makes a good death.
39. Actions speak louder than *the words.*	Actions speak louder than *words.*
40. Easier said *then* done.	Easier said *than* done.
41. Give *the dog* a bad name and hang him.	Give *a dog* a bad name and hang him.
42. You *can't* get something for nothing.	You *don't* get something for nothing.
43. Spare *your* rod and spoil your child.	Spare *the* rod and spoil the child.
44. Good clothes open all *the doors.*	Good clothes open all *doors.*
45. *Early* bird catches the worm.	*The* early bird catches the worm.
46. *The* first come, *the* first served.	*First* come, *first* served.
47. Better *be untaught* than ill taught.	Better *untaught* than ill taught.

INCORRECT	CORRECT
48. *Which* can't be cured, must be endured.	*What* can't be cured, must be endured.
49. *Sun* shines upon all alike.	*The sun* shines upon all alike.
50. *The example* is better than the precept.	*Example* is better than precept.
51. *You scratch* my back and I'll scratch yours.	*Scratch* my back and I'll scratch yours.
52. Empty vessels make *great* sound.	Empty vessels make *the greatest* sound.
53. Let *bygone* be *bygone*.	Let *bygones* be *bygones*.
54. *Friend* in need is friend indeed.	*A* friend in need is *a* friend indeed.
55. God helps *those who* help themselves.	God helps *those that* help themselves.
56. *Those* die well that live well.	*They* die well that live well.
57. *No* smoke without the fire.	*There's no* smoke without fire.
58. *The* habit is second nature.	*Habit* is second nature.
59. *The* laughter is the best medicine.	*Laughter* is the best medicine.
60. *Think* and *speak*.	*First think,* and *then speak.*
61. *See* before you leap.	*Look* before you leap.
62. Many hands make *the work lighter*.	Many hands make *light work*.
63. Honesty is *best* policy.	Honesty is *the best* policy.
64. A drowning man will clutch *a* straw.	A drowning man will clutch *at a* straw.
65. Standing *pool gathers* filth.	Standing *pools gather* filth.
66. An idle brain is *devil's* workshop.	An idle brain is *the* devil's workshop.

	INCORRECT	CORRECT
67.	Every man has *faults*.	Every man has *his faults*.
68.	No rose without *thorn*.	No rose without *a thorn*.
69.	Curiosity *kills* the cat.	Curiosity *killed* the cat.
70.	Mind your *business*.	Mind your *own business*.
71.	There are two sides *for* every question.	There are two sides *to* every question.
72.	Charity covers *multitude* of sins.	Charity covers *a multitude* of sins.
73.	All things are possible *for* God.	All things are possible *with* God.
74.	Nothing comes *from* nothing.	Nothing comes *of* nothing.
75.	*An opportunity* seldom knocks twice.	*Opportunity* seldom knocks twice.
76.	Make hay while *sun* shines.	Make hay while *the sun* shines.
77.	Look on the *brighter* side.	Look on the *bright* side.
78.	After *storm* comes *calm*.	After *a storm* comes *a calm*.
79.	Every cloud has *silver lining*.	Every cloud has *a silver lining*.
80.	*Man* is a lion in his own cause.	*A man* is a lion in his own cause.
81.	Never do things by *half*.	Never do things by *halves*.
82.	Patience is *virtue*.	Patience is *a virtue*.
83.	Where there is peace, *there is God*.	Where there is peace, *God is*.
84.	It takes two to make *quarrel*.	It takes two to make *a quarrel*.
85.	Birds of *same feathers* flock together.	Birds of *a feather* flock together.
86.	Barking dogs *never* bite.	Barking dogs *seldom* bite.
87.	Words cut *deeper* than swords.	Words cut *more* than swords.

INCORRECT	CORRECT
88. Keep something for *the rainy day*.	Keep something for *a rainy day*.
89. Time is *great healer*.	Time is *a great healer*.
90. There's no place like *the home*.	There is no place like *home*.
91. The proof of the pudding is in *eating*.	The proof of the pudding is in *the eating*.
92. A bad *worker* fights with his tools.	A bad *workman* fights with his tools.
93. A burnt *person* is afraid of fire.	A burnt *child* is afraid of fire.
94. *Like* king, *like* subjects.	*As the king, so are the* subjects.

SPELLING

WORDS COMMONLY MISSPELT

A

Abandon
Abatement
Abbreviation
Aberration
Abhor
Abhorrent
Ability
Abject
Abnormality
Abolition
Abridgement
Abscess
Absence
Absorb
Absorbent
Absurdity
Abundant
Abyss
Academy
Acceleration
Acceptable
Access
Accession

Accessory
Accident
Accidentally
Accommodate
Accommodation
Accompanying
Accomplice
Accomplish
Accomplishment
Account
Accountancy
Accrue
Accumulate
Accuse
Accustomed
Ache
Achievement
Acknowledgement
Acquaintance
Acquiesce
Acquit
Acre
Activities
Adaptation
Addiction

Adherent
Adjudication
Administration
Admission
Adolescent
Adulteration
Advantageous
Adventurous
Adversity
Advertisement
Advice (noun)
Advise (verb)
Aerial
Aerodrome
Aeroplane
Affection
Affliction
Affluent
Agency
Agglomerate
Aggravate
Aggregation
Agitation
Agnostic
Agreeable
Agricultural
Air
Alchemy
Alignment
All right
Allay
Allegation
Alleviate
Alley
Alliance
Allocation
Allopathy
Allowance
Allowed
Ally
Almost

Aloud
Alphabetical
Already
Altar
Alter
Aluminium
Amateur
Ambassador
Ambiguity
Ambiguous
Amendment
Amnesty
Amount
Analysis
Ancient
Anecdote
Anaesthetic
Angel
Angle
Ankle
Annihilate
Anniversary
Announcement
Annoyance
Anomalous
Anonymous
Answer
Antecedent
Anticipate
Antique
Anxiety
Anxious
Apology
Apparel
Appearance
Appendicitis
Appetite
Appraisal
Appreciate
Apprehension
Approachable

Appropriate
Approximation
Arbitrary
Archaeology
Architect
Arithmetic
Arm
Armour
Arrangement
Arrear
Arrived
Arrogance
Arrow
Article
Assassinate
Assessment
Assimilate
Astronomical
Ate
Attachment
Attempt
Attendant
Attention
Aunt
Auspicious
Authenticity
Author
Autobiography
Autumn
Auxiliary
Average
Awkward
Axe

B

Babies
Bachelor
Bacteria
Ballistic
Balloon

Bankruptcy
Banquet
Baptize
Barbarian
Bare
Barometer
Baron
Barren
Basin
Bath
Battery
Beam
Bear
Beautiful
Beginning
Behaviour
Beneath
Beneficial
Benefit
Benefited
Beseech
Besiege
Bibliography
Bilateral
Biscuit
Bitten
Blameable
Blandishment
Blew
Blister
Blockade
Blow
Blue
Blunder
Board
Bone
Booster
Bougainvillaea
Bough
Bourgeois
Bow

Bowl
Bracket
Brake
Bread
Break
Breast
Breathe
Bridge
Brief
Bristle
Bronchitis
Brought
Bruise
Buckle
Budget
Bugle
Build
Bulge
Bulletin
Bungalow
Buoyancy
Burden
Bureau
Bureaucracy
Burglary
Buried
Business
Buy

C

Cabbage
Cabinet
Cacophony
Cadence
Calculate
Calendar
Calibre
Calligraphy
Calm
Calorimeter

Camouflage
Campaign
Cancellation
Candidate
Canon
Cannon
Canvas
Canvass
Capability
Capillary
Capitalism
Capricious
Capsize
Captain
Captivity
Carburettor
Care
Career
Careful
Carefully
Careless
Carnage
Carpentry
Carried
Cartography
Castigate
Castle
Casual
Casualty
Catalogue
Cataract
Catch
Category
Caught
Causerie
Cavalry
Cease
Ceaseless
Ceiling
Celibacy
Cement

Cemetery	Clinical
Census	Clothes
Centenary	Cloud
Centralize	Coarse
Century	Coat
Ceramics	Cockroach
Ceremonial	Coerce
Ceremony	Coffee
Certainty	Cognizance
Certificate	Coherence
Cessation	Cohesion
Chair	Coincidence
Challenge	Collapse
Chameleon	Colleague
Champion	Collectivity
Chancellor	Collegiate
Chandelier	Colloquial
Character	Collusion
Chauvinism	Colonel
Chivalry	Colonialism
Chlorophyll	Colony
Cholera	Colour
Choose	Columnist
Chore	Commandant
Chronicle	Commemorate
Chronology	Commencement
Church	Commensurate
Cinema	Commercialise
Circle	Commission
Circumference	Committee
Citation	Commotion
Civilization (or Civilisation)	Communal
Clarity	Communalism
Classical	Communicate
Classification	Community
Claustrophobia	Company
Cleanser	Comparable
Clearance	Comparison
Cleavage	Compartment
Clemency	Compassion
Clerical	Compensation

Competition
Competitor
Complacency
Complainant
Complementary
Complexion
Complication
Complimentary
Composition
Compound
Comprehension
Compression
Compromise
Compulsory
Computation
Concealment
Conceit
Conceive
Concentration
Concession
Conciliate
Conclusion
Concurrence
Condolence
Condone
Conductor
Conference
Confession
Confiscate
Congenial
Congratulation
Conjunctivitis
Connoisseur
Connotation
Conquer
Conscience
Conscious
Consecutive
Consensus
Consequence
Considerable

Consignee
Conspiracy
Constellation
Constituency
Constitution
Construction
Consumption
Contagious
Contemptuous
Contiguous
Continental
Contingency
Continuance
Contrary
Controversy
Convalescence
Convenience
Conversation
Converse
Conviction
Coronation
Correlation
Correspondence
Corrigendum
Cosmopolitan
Cough
Could
Council
Counsel
Countenance
Counterfeit
Course
Courtesy
Cousin
Covenant
Crayon
Credential
Crematory
Cricketer
Crisis
Critical

Criticism
Crore
Crumble
Cure
Curiosity
Currant
Current
Cursory
Cycle

D

Dangerous
Dead
Dear
Decease
Deceit
Deceive
Decelerate
Decent
Decimal
Decision
Decompose
Deer
Defeated
Defensive
Deficiency
Definitely
Defraud
Deliberation
Delivered
Democracy
Demolition
Demonetise
Demonstration
Demurrage
Dense
Dependence
Depreciation
Depression
Descendant

Description
Desiccate
Despise
Destitute
Destruction
Detained
Detergent
Deteriorate
Determination
Deterrent
Detrimental
Devaluation
Deviation
Dew
Diabetes
Diagnose
Dialogue
Diameter
Diary
Dictator
Dietitian
Differentiable
Difficulty
Diminish
Diminutive
Diplomatic
Dirty
Disaffiliate
Disappear
Disciplinary
Discontinuity
Discotheque
Discourteous
Discover
Discrimination
Discussion
Disease
Disguise
Disintegrate
Dismount
Dispassionate

Dispensary
Dissatisfaction
Dissection
Disseminate
Dissimilarity
Dissociation
Dissolution
Dissolve
Distance
Distinction
Distinguish
Disturbance
Divergence
Diversion
Division
Divorce
Divulgence
Doctor
Documentary
Domestic
Dormitory
Draught
Drawn
Drought
Drunkard
Due
Dummy
Dungeon
Duplication
During
Dusty
Dwarf
Dwelling
Dyed
Dynamism
Dysentery
Dyspepsia

E

Eager

Eagle
Earn
Easily
Ebullient
Eccentric
Eclipse
Ecstasy
Editorial
Efficiency
Eighth
Elasticity
Electricity
Elegant
Elementary
Elephant
Eligibility
Emancipate
Embarrass
Embassy
Embezzlement
Emblem
Embrace
Embroidery
Emergency
Emeritus
Emigration
Eminence
Emission
Emolument
Emphasis
Empirical
Encouragement
Encyclopaedia
Endeavour
Endorsement
Engagement
Enhance
Enlightenment
Enmity
Enterprising
Entertainment

Hair
Hallucination
Handkerchiefs
Happened
Happily
Happiness
Harass
Hatred
Heal
Healthy
Heard
Heavily
Heinous
Heir
Hematosis
Hemorrhage
Here
Hereditary
Hesitation
Heterogeneity
Heterogeneous
Hideous
Hierarchy
Hindrance
Hinge
Hoarse
Hockey
Hole
Holiday
Homoepathy
Homogeneous
Homologous
Honest
Honestly
Honorarium
Honorary
Honour
Horizon
Horizontal
Horoscope
Horrible

Horror
Horse
Hospitality
Hostelry
Hostess
Hostility
Hour
Hourly
Hover
Howsoever
Humanitarian
Humanity
Humble
Humidity
Humiliation
Humour
Hundred
Hurdle
Hydrology
Hydroscope
Hygiene
Hypertension
Hypnotism
Hypocrisy
Hypotenuse
Hypothetical

I

Iconography
Idealism
Identical
Identity
Ideology
Idiomatic
Idiotic
Idle
Idol
Ignition
Ignominious
Ignorant

Ill-gotten
Illegality
Illegible
Illegitimate
Illicit
Illiteracy
Illiterate
Illogical
Illogicality
Illuminate
Illusion
Illusory
Illustrate
Illustration
Illustrious
Imaginary
Imagination
Imagine
Imitate
Imitation
Immaculate
Immaterial
Immaterialize
Immature
Immediate
Immediately
Immemorial
Immensity
Immerse
Immersion
Immigrant
Immigration
Imminence
Imminent
Immiscible
Immobility
Immolation
Immoral
Immorality
Immovable
Immunise

Immunity
Impartial
Impassionate
Impatience
Impeachment
Impediment
Imperative
Imperceptible
Imperial
Imperishable
Impersonal
Impersonation
Impertinent
Impervious
Implausible
Implicate
Implicit
Impolite
Impossibility
Impotent
Impregnate
Impression
Impressive
Imprisonment
Improvement
Inaccurate
Inadmissible
Inappropriate
Inattentive
Inaudible
Inauspicious
Incandescent
Incessant
Incidence
Incidental
Incipient
Inclement
Incognito
Incoherent
Incompatible
Incompetent

Enthusiasm
Entrance
Entrepreneur
Enumeration
Equatorial
Erosion
Erratic
Erroneous
Especially
Espionage
Essence
Essential
Etcetera
Eugenic
Evacuation
Evaporation
Evening
Evidence
Evince
Evolution
Exaggerate
Exalted
Examinee
Excellency
Exception
Excitement
Execution
Exempted
Exercise
Exhibition
Exist
Exonerate
Expatriate
Expectant
Expedite
Expenditure
Experience
Explicit
Expression
Extempore
Exterior

Extinction
Extinguish
Extracurricular
Extraneous
Extravagant
Extreme
Exuberant

F

Fabulous
Facility
Faculty
Familiarity
Fanatic
Fantastic
Farther
Fascinate
Fashionable
Favourite
Fear
Feature
February
Felicitate
Feverish
Fictitious
Fierce
Flabbergast
Flagrant
Flew
Flexible
Floor
Flour
Flourish
Flower
Forebode
Forecast
Foreword
Foreign
Foresee

Forfeit
Formality
Fracture
Fragrant
Fraternity
Frequency
Frequently
Friend
Frivolous
Fruit
Frustration
Fulfil
Fulfilled
Fulfilment
Fumble
Funeral
Furniture
Further
Future

G

Gadget
Gait
Galaxy
Gallantry
Gallery
Gamble
Garden
Gauge
Gelatinous
General
Generalize
Genetics
Genius
Gentleman
Genuine
Geography
Giant
Gingivitis
Glacier

Glamorous
Glorious
Glossary
Goal
Goes
Golden
Gone
Gonorrhea
Gorge
Government
Governor
Gracious
Gradient
Gradually
Graduate
Grammar
Granary
Gratification
Gratuitous
Gratuity
Gravitation
Graze
Grease
Greet
Grievance
Grieve
Grocery
Ground
Grown
Guarantee
Guarantor
Guidance
Gunnery
Gymkhana
Gymnastic
Gynaecology

H

Habitat
Habitual

Investigation
Invincible
Invulnerable
Irony
Irradiate
Irrationality
Irreconcilable
Irrecoverable
Irredeemable
Irregular
Irregularity
Irrelevant
Irreligious
Irrepressible
Irrespective
Irretrievable
Irreversible
Irrevocable
Irritability
Irritation
Italicise
Itinerary
Island
Issue

J

January
Jaundice
Jealous
Jealousy
Jeopardize
Jewelry
Jewellery
Joint
Joke
Journalism
Journalist
Journalistic
Journey
Jovial
Jubilant
Jubilation
Jubilee
Judge
Judgment
Judgement
Judicial
Judiciary
Judicious
Juggler
Jugglery
Juice
Junction
Jurist
Juror
Jury
Justiciable
Justifiable
Justification
Juvenile
Juxtaposition

K

Kaleidoscope
Kangaroo
Kernel
Kerosene
Kettle
Kindergarten
Kindliness
Kinematograph
Kingdom
Kitchen
Kite
Knead
Knife
Knight
Knitting
Knock
Knot

Knotty
Know
Knowledge
Knowledgeable

L

Label
Laboratory
Laborious
Lackadaisical
Lacklustre
Lacquer
Lacuna
Ladder
Lamb
Lament
Landscape
Language
Languish
Large
Lantern
Latch
Later
Lateral
Latitude
Laugh
Laughter
Laundry
Laureate
Laurel
Lavatory
Layer
Lazy
Lead
Leaf
League
Leaky
Learn
Leather
Leave

Lecturer
Legality
Legend
Legislator
Legislature
Legitimate
Leisure
Lenient
Lessen
Lesson
Lesser
Lettuce
Leukemia
Leukoderma
Level
Liable
Liaison
Libel
Liberalise
Liberty
Librarian
Licence (Noun)
License (verb)
Licentiate
Lieutenant
Light
Lightning
Likely
Lily
Limitation
Limousine
Lineage
Liquefaction
Literacy
Literally
Literary
Literature
Litigation
Little
Livable
Livelihood

Inconceivable
Incongruent
Inconsistent
Inconvenience
Incorrect
Incorruptible
Inconsistency
Incredible
Incredulous
Increment
Incumbent
Indecency
Indecision
Indefensible
Indefinite
Indelible
Indemnity
Indent
Independence
Indestructible
Indeterminate
Indian
Indication
Indifferent
Indigenous
Indigestion
Indiscipline
Indiscriminate
Indispensable
Indistinct
Individual
Individuality
Indivisible
Indorsee
Inducement
Inductance
Indulgence
Industrial
Inedible
Inefficiency
Ineligible

Inerrant
Inertia
Inessential
Inexhaustible
Inexpensive
Inexperienced
Infant
Infection
Infectious
Inference
Inferior
Infinite
Infinity
Infirmity
Inflammable
Inflation
Inflexible
Infliction
Influence
Influential
Influenza
Informality
Information
Infringement
Infuriate
Ingenious
Ingenuity
Inglorious
Ingratitude
Ingredient
Inhabitant
Inherent
Inherit
Inheritance
Inherited
Inhibition
Inhospitable
Inhumane
Initial
Initiate
Initiative

Injection
Injudicious
Injunction
Injurious
Injustice
Innate
Innocence
Innocent
Innovate
Innumerable
Inopportune
Inorganic
Inquire
Inquisition
Insensitive
Insight
Insignia
Insignificant
Insistent
Insolent
Insoluble
Insomnia
Inspiration
Instantaneous
Instantly
Instigate
Instinct
Institute
Instruction
Instrumental
Insubordinate
Insufficient
Insurance
Insurgency
Insurrection
Integrated
Intellectual
Intelligence
Intelligentsia
Intemperance
Intensify

Intension
Intensity
Intercept
Interchangeable
Intercommunication
Intercontinental
Interdisciplinary
Interesting
Interfacial
Interfere
Interference
Interior
Interjection
Intermediary
Intermediate
Intermission
Intermittent
International
Internment
Interplanetary
Interpolation
Interpretation
Interrelated
Interrogate
Interrupt
Interstitial
Intervene
Interview
Intimacy
Intolerable
Intolerant
Intravenous
Intrigue
Intrinsic
Introspection
Intrusion
Intuition
Invalidity
Invariant
Invasion
Inventory

Mythology

N

Naive
Narcotic
Narration
Nascent
Naturalise
Naturopathy
Naught
Navigation
Necessarily
Necessary
Necessity
Negligence
Negligible
Negotiable
Negotiation
Neighbourhood
Neither
Nemesis
Nervous
Neuropsychiatry
Neutrality
Nicety
Niche
Nineteenth
Ninetieth
Ninety
Ninth
Nobility
Noble
Noise
Nominal
Nominee
None
Nonsense
Non-violence
Normalcy
Notice

Noticeable
Notification
Nourishment
Novice
Nucleus
Nuisance
Numerator
Numerical
Numerology
Numerous
Nursery
Nurture
Nutrition
Nutritious

O

Oasis
Obedience
Obedient
Obituary
Objectionable
Obligation
Obligatory
Oblivion
Obnoxious
Obscene
Obscenity
Obscure
Obscurity
Observation
Observatory
Obsession
Obsolete
Obstacle
Obstetrics
Obstinacy
Obstruct
Obvious
Occasional
Occasionally

Occlusion
Occupancy
Occupation
Occupy
Ocean
O'clock
Octogenarian
Odour
Offence
Officialese
Officiate
Ointment
Oligarchy
Omelette
Omniscient
Once
Opaque
Open
Operation
Operative
Opinion
Ophthalmology
Opponent
Opportune
Opportunism
Opportunity
Opposite
Opposition
Oppressive
Optics
Optimist
Optimum
Opulence
Orator
Oratory
Orchard
Orchestra
Ordeal
Orderly
Ordinance
Ordinarily

Ordinary
Ordnance
Organism
Orgy
Oriental
Origin
Original
Originality
Originally
Ornament
Ornthology
Orphan
Orphanage
Orthodoxy
Orthography
Oscillation
Osmosis
Ostrich
Outlaw
Outrageous
Oval
Ovary
Oven
Override
Overrule
Overseer
Overwhelming

Pacify
Paddle
Pagan
Pageant
Palate
Palanquin
Pamper
Pancreas
Pane
Pain
Plain

Loaves
Locale
Locality
Longitude
Lottery
Lounge
Loyally
Loyalty
Lucrative
Luggage
Luminary
Luminescence
Luminosity
Luminous
Luncheon
Lustre
Lustrous
Luxurious
Luxury
Lyrist

M

Machine
Machinery
Made
Magazine
Magician
Magisterial
Magistery
Magnate
Magnet
Magnanimous
Magnificence
Magnitude
Maid
Maiden
Maintenance
Majesty
Majority
Malicious

Manageable
Managerial
Manicure
Manifestation
Manipulate
Mannerism
Manoeuvre
Mansion
Mantelpiece
Mantle
Manufacture
Manure
Manuscript
Marginal
Marketable
Marriageable
Marry
Marvellous
Martyr
Masculine
Massage
Massive
Mastery
Match
Material
Materialism
Maternity
Mathematician
Mathematics
Mattress
Maturity
Mean
Meant
Measles
Measure
Meat
Mechanical
Mechanician
Machanics
Mechanism
Mediation

Medicine
Medieval
Memorandum
Memorial
Meniscus
Menstrual
Menstruation
Merchandise
Merciful
Meridian
Meritorious
Merriment
Messenger
Metallurgy
Meteorology
Methodical
Methodology
Metrology
Metropolitan
Mice
Microphone
Migratory
Military
Millennia
Million
Millionaire
Mine
Miner
Mineral
Miniature
Minimum
Minor
Minority
Misbehaviour
Misbelief
Misbelieve
Miscellaneous
Mischievous
Misery
Misfortune
Misrepresent

Missionary
Mitosis
Mobility
Mockery
Moderate
Modernize
Modesty
Modification
Moisture
Modality
Molasses
Molecularity
Molestation
Momentarily
Moment
Momentary
Monarchy
Monopolize
Monotonous
Monumental
Morsel
Mortality
Mortgage
Mortification
Mortuary
Mosquito
Mountain
Mountainous
Mourn
Moustache
Movable
Multilingual
Multimillionaire
Multiplication
Mumble
Municipality
Muscle
Musician
Mystery
Mysterious
Mysticism

Rode
Roller
Rostrum
Rough
Rude
Rupee
Rupture
Rural
Rye

S

Sabbath
Sacrilege
Safely
Saffron
Sagacious
Sale
Sail
Saliva
Sanatorium
Satire
Sauce
Saviour
Saw
Scandal
Scarce
Scavenger
Scenery
Schedule
Science
Scissors
Scorpion
Scoundrel
Scuffle
Search
Secular
Sedulous
Sense
Sensual
Separate

Serious
Several
Shuttle
Sign
Signatory
Siesta
Sieve
Simultaneous
Slaughter
Sneeze
Soap
Sole
Soul
Sought
Spade
Speculate
Spontaneous
Square
Stationary
Stationery
Steal
Steel
Sublimate
Suffrage
Suit
Superior
Surprise
Suspicion
Suspicious
Sweat
Sycophant
Sympathy
Syringe
Syrup

T

Taboo
Tablet
Tantamount
Tariff

Technical
Telephone
Television
Temperature
Temporary
Terminology
Territory
Tetanus
Theatre
Theory
Thief
Thorough
Thought
Threw
Throne
Through
Throw
Tincture
Together
Tongue
Total
Totalitarian
Touch
Tournament
Towel
Travel
Traveller
Treat
Truly
Trumpet
Tuesday
Tuition
Tunnel
Turmoil
Turtle
Twelfth
Twelve
Twice
Tycoon
Typhoid
Typical

Tyrant
Tyranny
Tyre

U

Ugly
Ulcer
Umpire
Unaccountable
Uncle
Unconscious
Undermine
Unicameral
Uniform
Unique
Universe
Urine
Usual
Usurp
Usury
Utensil
Utility
Utopia

Vacation
Vaccinate
Vacillate
Vain
Valley
Valour
Vandalism
Vein
Velvet
Venereal
Vengeance
Veranda
Vermilion
Versus

Plane
Panorama
Paragon
Parallel
Paralysis
Paramour
Parasite
Parochial
Parry
Parrot
Particle
Particularly
Partner
Pasture
Pathos
Pattern
Pavilion
Peace
Peacefully
Pear
Pecuaiary
Pedal
Peddle
Pedestrian
Pence
Pencil
Pension
Pepper
Perch
Perfidy
Perquisite
Permeate
Persecute
Persevere
Perspective
Personnel
Personal
Pessimism
Phantom
Phenomenon
Philanthropy

Physiology
Physique
Piece
Piety
Pique
Pivot
Placard
Planetarium
Pleasant
Plebiscite
Poetry
Porter
Pour
Practice (noun)
Practise (verb)
Prayers
Precious
Preliminary
Preparation
Preposition
Prerogative
Present
Pressure
Priest
Principal
Principle
Prior
Profane
Progeny
Programme
Proletariat
Proliferate
Propeller
Prophecy (noun)
Prophesy (verb)
Proprietor
Proximate
Psychic
Psychology
Puberty
Punctual

Puncture
Pursue
Purview
Pyorrhoea

Q

Quack
Quality
Quantity
Quarrel
Quarrelled
Qualify
Quarantine
Quarter
Queen
Queer
Quell
Quest
Question
Queue
Quibble
Quick
Quip
Quiet
Quite
Quit
Quiver
Quiz
Quota
Quotation
Quote
Quotient

R

Rabies
Radio
Radiate
Radium
Raffle

Raid
Rally
Random
Rascal
Rational
Reader
Realm
Rebellion
Receipt
Recent
Reckon
Recognize
Recoil
Reconnaisance
Reconnoitre
Recreation
Redundant
Referee
Reflex
Refrigerator
Rehabilitate
Reign
Rein
Reinstate
Reiterate
Release
Relief
Relieved
Religion
Remembrance
Renaissance
Repair
Require
Resourceful
Resurrection
Retaliate
Retrospect
Revenue
Rhyme
Right
Road

Vertical
Vessel
Vicarious
Vicinity
Vicissitude
View
Vigour
Villain
Virtue
Vision
Visitor
Voice
Volte-face
Voluntary
Voyage
Vulture

W

Wad
Wade
Waft
Wafter
Wagon
Waist
Wait
Wander
Warrant
Waste
Wear
Weather
Week
Weigh
Weight
Were
Where
Whether
Whiff
White
Whole
Will-o'-the-wisp

Wisdom
Wizard
Wonder
Wood
Would
Wreath
Wrest
Wretch
Wriggle
Wrinkle
Writ
Wrong

X

Xerography
Xenophobia

Y

Yacht
Year
Yearn
Yellow
Yelp
Yeoman
Yesterday
Yield
Yokel
Yolk
Young
Yours

Z

Zealously
Zebra
Zenith
Zigzag
Zodiac
Zoology

WORDS WHICH SHOULD NOT BE JOINED

CORRECT	INCORRECT
None the less	Nonetheless
All right	Alright
All round	Allround
At once	Atonce
At least	Atleast
In spite of	Inspite of
Up till	Uptill
Some time	Sometime
Well done	Welldone
No one	Noone
Up to	Upto

WORDS WHICH SHOULD NOT BE SEPARATED

CORRECT	INCORRECT
Anyhow	Any how
Anything	Any thing
Almost	All most
Already	All ready
Anybody	Any body
Afterwards	After wards
Cannot	Can not
Everybody	Every body
Everywhere	Every where
Elsewhere	Else where
However	How ever
Into	In to
Instead of	In stead of
Madman	Mad Man
Moreover	More over
Notwithstanding	Not with standing
Nobody	No body

CORRECT	INCORRECT
Newspaper	News paper
Ourselves	Our selves
Otherwise	Other wise
Outside	Out side
Sometimes	Some times
Somebody	Some body
Schoolboy	School boy
Somehow	Some how
Together	To gether
Today	To day
Tomorrow	To morrow
Utmost	Ut most
Welfare	Well fare
Welcome	Well come
Wherever	Where ever
Anyone	Any one
Everyone	Every one
Meanwhile	Mean while

WORDS COMMONLY CONFUSED

Accept	:	She could not *accept* my invitation.
Except	:	Everybody attended the meeting *except* the chairman.
Advice	:	Amit followed his father's good *advice*.
Advise	:	He doesn't *advise* me anymore.
Affect	:	His criticism doesn't *affect* me now.
Effect	:	Your advice had a lasting *effect* on her.
Access	:	He has no *access* to the boss.
Excess	:	He eats, drinks and smokes to *excess*.
Adapt	:	He was quick to *adapt* himself to the new place.
Adept	:	She is *adept* at public relations.
Adopt	:	He has been slow to *adopt* our recommendations.
Allowed	:	You are *allowed* to see the principal now.
Aloud	:	He spoke *aloud* so that all could hear.
Altar	·	He placed his offerings at the *altar*.
Alter	:	The boss is not willing to *alter* his decision.

Angel	:	She is such an *angel*, nobody would want to hurt her.
Angle	:	I couldn't see her from that *angle*.
Abject	:	His *abject* poverty keeps him from meeting people
Object	:	This new water pump is an *object* of curiosity among the villagers.
Allusion	:	He did not make a single *allusion* to the scandal in his speech.
Illusion	:	It is an *illusion* to think he did not take the bribe.
Amiable	:	Shaila is an *amiable* person.
Amicable	:	They resolved their differences and came to an *amicable* settlement.
Assent	:	The chairman has given his *assent* to our proposal.
Ascent	:	The hotel is at the top of the hill and the *ascent* is rather steep.
Accent	:	I was confused by his Australian *accent*.
Bear	:	With all that overgrown hair he looked like a *bear*.
Bear	:	I can't *bear* to see her suffer like this.
Bare	:	The champion ran the last lap of his race *bare*footed.
Beer	:	*Beer* is the most popular drink in this city.
Berth	:	I couldn't get my *berth* reserved on this train.
Birth	:	The *birth* of a child has brought joy into their lives.
Born	:	He was *born* in our village.
Borne	:	She has *borne* many trials in life.
Break	:	He could easily *break* the glass.
Brake	:	By the time he applied the *brakes*, it was too late.

Bridle	:	He couldn't control the horse because it was without a *bridle*.
Bridal	:	Her *bridal* dress was imported from England.
Bail	:	He has just been released on *bail*.
Bale	:	He has about a thousand *bales* of cotton in stock.
Bath	:	She has her *bath* after the morning walk.
Bathe	:	We *bathe* in the river for fun.
Beneficial	:	The vocations in the hills have proved *beneficial* to my health.
Beneficent	:	The *beneficent* king was loved by his subjects.
Beside	:	She sat *beside* him during the concert.
Besides	:	*Besides* all the directors there will be a few observers present at today's meeting.
Boar	:	The wild *boar* can be a destructive animal.
Bore	:	I was *bored* at yesterday's party.
Bore	:	She *bore* three children before she died.
Canvas	:	She was wearing the common *canvas* shoes.
Canvass	:	I have decided to *canvass* for Pradeep during the forthcoming elections.
Check	:	The authorities have failed to *check* the uncontrolled growth of the slums.
Cheque	:	The *cheque* he issued was not in any favour.
Ceiling	:	There is a *ceiling* on buying of land in this stage.
Sealing	:	He is busy *sealing* the envelopes.

Compliment	:	She blushed at his *compliment*.
Complement	:	An angle of 30 degrees is the *complement* of an angle of 60 degrees.
Corporal	:	No one today tolerates *corporal* punishment in schools.
Corporeal	:	Fairies have no *corporeal* existence.
Clothes	:	You need light woollen *clothes* during this part of the year.
Cloth	:	The *cloth* I bought today was of a very poor quality.
Continually	:	He has been touring *continually* for the past two years.
Continuously	:	It has been raining *continuously* for the past five hours.
Credible	:	Her story was not *credible*.
Creditable	:	He is handicapped, therefore, his victory is all the more *creditable*.
Council	:	He is a member of the student's *council*.
Counsel	:	He had to suffer because he did not give heed to his father's *counsel*.
Current	:	The *current* of the river is very strong at this point.
Current	:	We discussed the *current* affairs of the company.
Currant	:	*Currants* are among my favourite dry-fruits.
Dairy	:	He works on a *dairy* farm.
Diary	:	He has a habit of noting everything down in his *diary*.

Dependant	:	We employed her because she has no *dependants*.
Dependent	:	He is *dependent* on the industrialist for all the finances.
Dear	:	As prices rise, things are getting to be *dear*.
Dear	:	Everything you have given is *dear* to my heart
Deer	:	The *deer* have found protection in this sanctuary.
Disease	:	He is not aware of the *disease* afflicting him.
Decease	:	No one was bothered about the *deceased* man; they were fighting over his property.
Difference	:	There is a *difference* between what you say and what you do.
Deference	:	He is very polite to his teachers and treats them with great *deference*.
Dose	:	The doctor advised him to take a *dose* of medicine at bedtime.
Doze	:	I *dozed* off to sleep during the long speech.
Elicit	:	The police could *elicit* no information from the dying terrorist.
Illicit	:	He has been arrested for *illicit* trade practices.
Eligible	:	He is *eligible* for promotion this year.
Illegible	:	Her handwriting is *illegible*
Eminent	:	He is among the *eminent* scientists of the country.
Imminent	:	He is in a coma and his death seems *imminent*.
Fair	:	I bought this shawl at the *fair*.
Fair	:	She is proud of her *fair* complexion.

Fare	:	There is likely to be a hike in air *fares* in the next budget.
Fare	:	I have not *fared* too badly in my interview.
Facility	:	There is no booking *facility* at his office.
Felicity	:	She finds real *felicity* in the service of suffering humanity.
Floor	:	Don't leave things lying about on the *floor*.
Flour	:	We buy our wheat *flour* from the mill.
Flowers	:	Don't pluck *flowers* from the public parks.
Faint	:	He *fainted* after the tough fight.
Feint	:	There is a *feint* hope of his recovery.
Goal	:	He doesn't seem to have a *goal* in life.
Gaol	:	He has been sent to *gaol* for his crimes.
Gamble	:	He goes to the casino to *gamble*.
Gambol	:	He saw the children *gamboling* in the rain.
Hair	:	Your *hair* needs a lot of care.
Hare	:	The *hare* is a timid animal.
Heir	:	He is the natural *heir* to his father's property.
Hale	:	When I last saw him he was *hale* and hearty.
Hail	:	She *hails* from the southern part of this state.
Hail	:	It *hailed* during the night.
Heal	:	He wounds are rather serious and will take a long time to *heal*.
Heel	:	When the lady raised an alarm the chain-snatcher took to his *heels*.

Heard	:	I have *heard* this story before.
Herd	:	A *herd* of wild elephants was seen at the edge of the forest.
Hole	:	Rabbits live in *holes*.
Whole	:	He did not let him relate the *whole* story.
Industrial	:	This being an *industrial* town it is highly polluted.
Industrious	:	He is always successful because he is *industrious* by nature.
Insight	:	His deep *insight* into human nature makes him a successful story writer.
Incite	:	He is accused of *inciting* the crowds to run violent.
Later	:	The principal said I could see him *later*.
Latter	:	The *latter* part of your letter is depressing.
Letter	:	Your *letter* arrived when I was away.
Lose	:	He as afraid of *losing* her in the crowd.
Loose	:	She is known for her *loose* character.
Leave	:	Let me take *leave* of you now.
Leave	:	Our train is expected to *leave* the station at 12.00 noon.
Live	:	If you want to *live* in this house, you must behave yourself.
Medal	:	He has won a *medal* for topping the class.
Meddle	:	I do not believe in *meddling* in others' affairs.
Miner	:	A *miner* was trapped in the mine yesterday.
Minor	:	Tina is still a *minor* and cannot exercise voting rights.

Naughty	:	He was punished because he was *naughty*.
Knotty	:	He discovered that the problem of taking bribes was really *knotty*.
None	:	*None* of the directors came for the meeting.
Nun	:	*Nuns* have succeeded in maintaining discipline in their school.
Order	:	The government *order* on the closure of liquor shops comes into effect next month.
Odour	:	The *odour* emanating from the room made me feel sick.
Ardour	:	I am amazed at the youthful *ardour* displayed by your grandfather even at this age.
Pare	:	I need a knife to *pare off* this mango.
Pear	:	My orchard has a few *pear* trees.
Pair	:	Get me a *pair* of scissors.
Patrol	:	The police officer was on *patrol* when the crime was committed.
Petrol	:	*Petrol* has become costlier since the last budget.
Peace	:	The *peace* of the village is broken since the last elections.
Piece	:	I was surprised to see *pieces* of broken glass on the floor.
Plane	:	The *plane* took off on schedule.
Plain	:	The Gangetic *plain* receives very moderate rainfall.
Plain	:	Don't be deceived by her *plain* looks.
Practice	:	He lost the match because he was short of *practice*.
Practise	:	They have been *practising* their play for the past one month.

Principal	:	You may meet the *principal* of our college after two in the afternoon.
Principal	:	He was the *principal* speaker at the debate.
Principle	:	It is against his *principles* to admit children recommended by politicians.
Pray	:	We have come to the temple to *pray*.
Prey	:	The cat played with its *prey* before killing it.
Price	:	I was not too happy with the *price* of this book.
Prize	:	Everyone expected him to win the *prize* for acting.
Pore	:	The little holes in your skin are called *pores*.
Poor	:	She has decided to spend her life working for the *poor*.
Pour	:	He *poured* cold water over his burns.
Princes	:	Cricket was very popular among the Indian *princes*.
Princess	:	The king was unhappy about the choice of the *princess*.
Precedent	:	If I make an advance payment of your salary this month, you must not take it as a *precedent*, because I shall not do the same again.
President	:	The meeting was chaired by the *president* of the party.
Quiet	:	He is *quiet* by nature.
Quit	:	In spite of his success he had to *quit* the job.
Quite	:	She is *quite* popular among her colleagues.
Right	:	You were *right* when you said the company would get a bad name because of its present policies.
Rite	:	He doesn't seem to give much importance to the religious *rites* associated with marriage.

Write	:	*Write* out your application on a clean sheet of paper.
Wright	:	Everyone knows that you are a good play *wright*.
Route	:	I am not familiar with this bus *route*.
Root	:	He is determined to *root* out all corruption from this organisation.
Rout	:	The visiting team was *routed* by the home team.
Seam	:	Her skirt was giving way at the *seams*.
Seem	:	She *seems* quite familiar.
Sight	:	She was shocked at the *sight* of destruction caused by the fire.
Site	:	This is the *site* of our new factory.
Cite	:	She *cited* a verse from her book.
Soar	:	The *soaring* prices of essential commodities have made life difficult for the poor.
Sore	:	At the end of the twenty-kilometre walk my feet were *sore*.
Stationary	:	The express train rammed into the *stationary* goods train.
Stationery	:	He is in the habit of using office *stationery* for his personal work.
Senses	:	He has come to his *senses* now that a lot of damage has been done to his reputation.
Census	:	She was not born when the last *census* were taken.
Tamper	:	By now, he knows who *tampered* with the office records.
Temper	:	He is never known to lose his *temper*.

Taste	:	He was *tasting* that drink for the first time.
Test	:	He thought he wouldn't pass the *test*.
Team	:	The *team* has done well under your captaincy.
Teem	:	The site of the train accident was *teeming* with people when I arrived.
Vain	:	All his efforts to prove his innocence before the board were in *vain*.
Vane	:	The *vane* is pointing towards the south.
Vein	:	The bleeding wouldn't stop because he had cut a *vein*.
Vale	:	After driving trough the beautiful *vale* we came to a town.
Veil	:	She had covered her face with a *veil*.
Wail	:	The women gathered around the dead man were *wailing*.
Way	:	The *way* to the temple was through a forest.
Weigh	:	*Weigh* the bags before loading them.
Wet	:	We walked on the *wet* sand.
Whet	:	The sight of delicious food *whetted* our appetite.
Wave	:	He stopped when I *waved* out to him.
Wave	:	When we saw the *waves* rising we decided it was time to swim in the sea.
Waive	:	The principal has *waived* my fees for this month.
Whether	:	I asked *whether* she would join us.
Weather	:	We chose to go out because the *weather* was fine.

Weak	:	The old man was too *weak* to walk.
Week	:	She visits me every *week*.
Wick	:	The lamp needed a new *wick*.
Wonder	:	I *wonder* if the boss will be true to his promises.
Wander	:	Why don't you do some work instead of *wandering* about the place?

INAPPROPRIATE USE OF WORDS

INCORRECT	CORRECT
1. Don't *cut* from the left side.	Don't *overtake* from the left side.
2. Please *open* the light.	Please *turn* on the light.
3. You may *shut* off the light.	You may *turn* off the light.
4. He is struggling for breath, *open* his clothing.	He is struggling for breath, *loosen* his clothing.
5. There was a *cut* in the queue.	There was a *break* in the queue.
6. Initially, I had no intention of *spending for* him.	Initially, I had no intention of *paying* for him.
7. No one expected him to *bluff* his parents.	No one expected him to *lie* to his parents.
8. I am amazed at the *cheap* prices of electronic goods here.	I am amazed at the *low* prices of electronic goods here.
9. I liked the way you *fired* at him.	I liked the way you *criticized/scolded* him.
10. We *wished* as he entered the room.	We *greeted him* as he entered the room.
11. *Last time* you were in a different department.	*Previously* you were in a different department.

INCORRECT	CORRECT
12. *Last time* we had a lot more benefits in this company.	*In the past* we had a lot more benefits in this company.
13. *I feel bad* to see him suffer like he does.	*It pains* me to see him suffering like this.
14. I am sorry to *know* you lost your father.	I am sorry to *learn* you lost your father.
15. How did you *know* that Ravi had left the place?	How did you *find out* that Ravi had left the place?
16. She forgot to *give* her assignment on time.	She forgot to *hand in* her assignment on time.
17. *At last* he reached his destination.	*Finally,* he reached his destination.
18. She is *undergoing* a course in hairstyling at this institute.	She is *taking* a course in hairstyling at this institute.
19. We *stay* at 69, Park Avenue, Madras.	We *live* at 69, Park Avenue, Madras.
20. She is still *schooling*.	She is still at *school*.
21. You should not expect her to *follow* you to the city.	You should not expect her to *accompany* you to the city.
22. I prefer a *sir* to be my guide.	I prefer a *male teacher* to be my guide.
23. She could not *avoid* the house being sold.	She could not *prevent* the house being sold.
24. This feels like a furnace after the *cooling* climate of the hills.	This feels like a furnace after the *cool* climate of the hills.
25. I gave her a *ride* to office yesterday.	I gave her a *lift* to office yesterday.
26. You can *put up* with me at the hostel.	You can *stay* with me at the hostel.

INCORRECT	CORRECT
27. On weekends she goes *marketing* with her friends.	On weekends she goes *shopping* with her friends.
28. You have not cared to consider the other *aspect*.	You have not cared to consider the other *point of view*.
29. Haven't you *called* your colleagues to the dinner?	Haven't you *invited* your colleagues to the dinner?
30. He can write all the *alphabets*.	He can write all the *letters of the alphabet*.
31. The Principal *scolded* him for his role in the demonstration.	The Principal *reprimanded* him for his role in the demonstration.
32. She prefers *slippers* to shoes.	She prefers *sandals* to shoes.
33. You may *sleep* after you have finished your homework.	You may *go to sleep/bed* after you have finished your homework.
34. I'm *so* sorry I hurt your feelings.	I am *very* sorry I hurt your feelings.
35. I *took food* at a highway restaurant.	I *ate* at a highway restaurant.
36. He had *taken a meal* before he left.	He had *had a meal* before he left.
37. She saw me in the *compound*.	She saw me in the *garden*.
38. Are you still *attached to the* UNICEF?	Are you still *working for the* UNICEF?
39. I'll *pay for your dinner* today.	I'll *treat you to a dinner* today.
40. You will find most of the stocks in the *godown*.	You will find most of the stocks in the *warehouse*.
41. You will find him in the school *compound*.	You will find him on the school *premises*.
42. We *went to see a show* last night.	We *went to see a film* last night.

INCORRECT	CORRECT
43. He was *on leave* in the hills.	He was *on a holiday* in the hills.
44. She won't *friend me* because I did not lend her my book.	She won't *be friends with me* because I did not lend her my book.
45. I shall *send* you to the airport.	I shall *take* you to the airport.
46. Examinations are not the best way of assessing students; they should, therefore, be *cancelled*.	Examinations are not the best way of assessing students; they should, therefore, be *abolished*.
47. Some workers have become a *waste* to their employers.	Some workers have become a *liability* to their employers.
48. Population explosion is one of our *biggest* problems.	Population explosion is one of our *chief* problems.
49. These days, we find women in many occupations which were once *reserved* for men.	These days, we find women in many occupations which were once *preserved* for men.
50. These days a university degree is considered the main *qualification* for getting a job.	These days a university degree is considered the main *criterion* for getting a job.
51. The rights of the minorities are *preserved* by our Constitution.	The rights of the minorities are *protected* by our Constitution.
52. Advertising *encourages* people to buy things.	Advertising *influences* people to buy things.
53. If more and more people take up self-employment we can *settle* our unemployment problem to some extent.	If more and more people take up self-employment we can *overcome* our unemployment problem to some extent.
54. If your have done wrong you are *subject* to punishment.	If you have done wrong you are *liable* to punishment.
55. Mother Teresa has *spent* her life in the service of the destitute.	Mother Teresa has *dedicated* her life to the service of the destitute.

INCORRECT	CORRECT
56. One question which *surfaces/rises* is how far the management would be willing to implement our proposals.	One question which *arises* is how far the management would be willing to implement our proposals.
57. The principal has expressed his *anxiety* about the falling standards of discipline.	The principal has expressed his *concern* about the falling standards of discipline.
58. many workers are *innocent* about their duties towards the company.	Many workers are *ignorant* about their duties towards the company.
59. Those who were *effected* by the earthquake have been rehabilitated.	Those who were *affected* by the earthquake have been rehabilitated.
60. Those who were injured in the accident were sent to the hospital to be *revived*.	Those who were injured in the accident were sent to the hospital to be *treated*.
61. Our teenagers appear to have *deserted* their own culture and preferred the western way of life.	Our teenagers appear to have *rejected* their own culture and preferred the western culture.
62. They migrated to Australia in the hope of finding a better *status* of living.	They migrated to Australia in the hope of finding a better *standard* of living.
63. Singapore has *arisen* as one of the most industrialised countries	Singapore has *emerged* as one of the most industrialised countries.
64. I have agreed to co-operate with the police in their *endeavour/effort*.	I have agreed to co-operate with the police in their *investigation*.
65. Rustication *prevents* students from indulging in offensive ragging.	Rustication *deters* student from indulging in offensive ragging.

INCORRECT	CORRECT
66. That operation was quite complicated and could not be *done* here.	That operation was quite complicated and could not be *performed* here.
67. Advertisements are meant to inform us about the *item*.	Advertisements are meant to inform us about the *product*.
68. You seem to be one of those who work hard to *spread* your religion.	You seem to one of those who work hard to *propagate* your religion.
69. Beggars could not be *selectors*.	Beggars could not be *choosers*.
70. Future events *show* their shadows.	Future events *cast* their shadows.
71. Cut your *shirt* according to your cloth.	Cut your *coat* according to your cloth.
72. *Practice* is better than preaching.	*Example* is better than precept.
73. Half *bread* is better than no bread.	Half *a loaf* is better than no bread.
74. It is no use to *weep* over *lost* milk.	It is no use *crying* over *spilt* milk.
75. You cannot clap with one hand.	It takes two to make a quarrel.
76. Son is like father.	Like father, like son.

PUNCTUATION

INCORRECT	CORRECT

The Commas

1. Anika your best friend is leaving the college.

   Anika, your best friend, is leaving the college.

2. You are aware I'm sure that everyone in the hostel wants you to stay.

   You are aware, I'm sure, that everyone in the hostel wants you to stay.

3. She is I hope our best bet for the singles competition.

   She is, I hope, our best bet for the singles competition.

4. I've alway's treated her views as a matter of fact with great respect.

   I've always treated her views, as a matter of fact, with great respect.

5. The director says the teacher is ill-informed.

   The director, says the teacher, is ill-informed.

6. 'I want you, Prema to leave the class' announced the teacher.

   'I want you, Prema, to leave the class,' announced the teacher.

7. Prema replied 'I will do so.'

   Prema replied, 'I will do so.'

8. I therefore request you to kindly grant me one day's leave.

   I, therefore, request to kindly grant me one day's casual leave.

9. Putting down her suitcase the girl chased the pickpocket.

   Putting down her suitcase, the girl chased the pickpocket.

INCORRECT	CORRECT
10. However the function ended in a total chaos.	However, the function ended in a total chaos.
11. Pamela our representative at the conference is a brilliant girl.	Pamela, our representative at the conference, is a brilliant girl.
12. The captain of the victorious team who was waiting for his turn now came up to the stage.	The captain of the victorious team, who was waiting for his turn, now came up to the stage.
13. Manoj the son of our chairman has just taken over as the managing director.	Manoj, the son of our chairman, has just taken over as the managing director.
14. This is Praveen my secretary who attends to all my office matters.	This is Praveen, my secretary, who attends to all my office matters.
15. Bangalore the garden city of India is getting overcrowded.	Bangalore, the garden city of India, is getting overcrowded.
16. Your mother I'm sure will not approve of this idea.	Your mother, I'm sure, will not approve of this idea.
17. Ashok we all believed was on our side.	Ashok, we all believed, was on our side.
18. Karan and Amar and Kavita visited us yesterday.	Karan, Amar and Kavita visited us yesterday.
19. You spoke in a rude tone of voice which is not the way in which to speak to a father.	You spoke in a rude tone of voice, which is not the way in which to speak to a father.
20. I saw a lean man with an umbrella waiting outside your gate.	I saw a lean man with an umbrella, waiting outside your gate.
21. I saw a man who was lean and had an umbrella in his hand waiting outside your gate.	I saw a man, who was lean and had an umbrella in his hand, waiting outside your gate.
22. The school in which I study, is on a hill.	The school in which I study is on a hill.

INCORRECT	CORRECT
23. If you have done wrong you better make a clean breast of it so that you have no regrets when you think of the past.	If you have done wrong, you better make a clean breast of it, so that you have no regrets, when you think of the past.
24. Moreover I live in this very colony.	Moreover, I live in this very colony.
25. Furthermore I helped him get a job.	Furthermore, I helped him get a job.
26. Nevertheless come to my show.	Nevertheless, come to my show.
27. In addition Yoga is said to relieve many common ailments.	In addition, Yoga is said to relieve many common ailments.

☞ NOTES

1. The most usual occasions when we use commas are five:
    a) Round a parenthesis or a phrase, especially when either occurs in the middle of a sentence grammatically complete without phrases, especially participle, placed at the beginning of a sentence.
    b) Round words in apposition and the name of the person addressed in direct speech.
    c) When inverted commas open and close.
    d) Round relative clauses when the relative pronoun is doing the work of a conjunction also.
    e) Round a subordinate clause in a sentence.
2. There are also occasions when a comma is obviously required because the absence of one may lead to the wrong words being read together.
3. The short relative clause, purely adjectival in effect, sandwiched between two parts of a sentence, does not need commas.
4. When it is possible to substitute the word 'that' for the relative pronoun without loss of idiom or a change of meaning, the relative clause should not have commas at all.

INCORRECT	CORRECT

Full Stop

	INCORRECT	CORRECT
1.	The departure time of the superfast train is 4 am	The departure time of the superfast trains is 4 a.m.
2.	You just wait here The bus will come	You just wait here. The bus will come.
3.	Wait for a while He may come in at any moment now.	Wait for a while. He may come in at any moment now.
4.	A mere MA in English is not enough to get you this job.	A mere M.A. is not enough to get you this job.
5.	Dr P Pawar is a leading cardiologist.	Dr. P. Pawar is a leading cardiologist.
6.	I have not seen you before I'm in a hurry I can't see you now.	I have not seen you before. I'm in a hurry. I can't see you now.
7.	He is a student of our college He is known to be good speaker.	He is a student of our college. He is known to be a good speaker.

Apostrophe

	INCORRECT	CORRECT
1.	The *principals* daughter is joining us on the staff.	The *principal's* daughter is joining us on the staff.
2.	We spent the evening in the *childrens* park.	We spent the evening in the *children's* park.
3.	He seems to be interested in someone *elses* property.	He seems to be interested in someone *else's* property.
4.	The *teachers* hostel is close to the *students* hostel.	The *teacher's* hostel is close to the *students'* hostel.
5.	You have no business to laugh at *someones* misfortunes	You have no business to laugh at *someone's* misfortunes.
6.	She is involved with several *womens* organisations.	She is involved with several *women's* organisations.

	INCORRECT	CORRECT
7.	For *Mosess* sake we postponed our party.	For *Moses'* sake we postponed our party.
8.	When the *cats* away, the mice will play.	When the *cat's* away, the mice will play.
9.	*Bachelors* wives and *maids* children are well taught.	*Bachelors'* wives and *maids'* children are well taught.
10.	*Wont* you come with me?	*Won't* you come with me?

Semicolon

	INCORRECT	CORRECT
1.	The frame of the window was made of fine black ebony, and as she was looking out, she pricked her finger.	The frame of the window was made of black ebony; and as she was looking out, she pricked her finger.
2.	This queen died, and the king married another wife, who was very beautiful.	This queen died; and the king married another wife, who was very beautiful.
3.	Then the servant led the princess away, but his heart melted when she begged him to spare her life.	Then the servant led the princess away; but his heart melted when she begged him to spare her life.
4.	The dwarfs went out all day long to do their work, seeking for gold in the mountains, but Snow White remained at home, and they warned her.	The dwarfs went out all day long to do their work, seeking for gold in the mountains; but Snow White remained at home; and they warned her.
5.	Your hair is black mine is brown.	Your hair is black; mine is brown.
6.	Some men eat that they may live, others live that they may eat.	Some men eat that they may live; others live that they may eat.
7.	Reading maketh a full man, conference, a ready man, writing an exact man.	Reading maketh a full man; conference, a ready man; writing, an exact man.

Hyphen

INCORRECT	CORRECT
1. The *passersby* ignored the beggar.	The *passers-by* ignored the beggar.
2. Our *exprincipal* has won a national award.	Our *ex-principal* has won a national award.
3. I have requested for a *reevaluation* of my answer papers.	I have requested for a *re-evaluation* of my answer papers.
4. Arun Lal is a *self made* person.	Arun Lal is a *self-made* person.
5. We spent most of our holiday in a *boat house*.	We spent most of our holiday in a *boat-house*.
6. She lives here alone with her *mother in law*.	She lives here alone with her *mother-in-law*.
7. He looks rather young for his *forty six* years.	He looks rather young for his *forty-six* years.
8. *Two thirds* of our population is still poor.	*Two-thirds* of our population is still poor.

Dash

1. "Well," said Poo-Poo's mother, "that's very nice, but,"	"Well," said Poo-Poo's mother, "that's very nice, but —."
2. Mr. Wigg was looking at Mary Poppins, a curious look, half-amused, half-accusing.	Mr. Wigg was looking at Mary Poppins — a curious look, half-amused, half-accusing.
3. 'No, but I, I, oh? Eeyore, I burst the balloon!'	'No, but — I— I— oh, Eeyore, I burst the balloon!'
4. Never again did he chase a mouse, except for fun.	Never again did he chase a mouse — except for fun.
5. Hans, for this was the name of the apprentice, was always hungry.	Hans — for this was the name of the apprentice — was always hungry.

INCORRECT	CORRECT
6. I am able to keep myself invisible by an exercise of will-power, an exceedingly exhausting job, and I can keep you invisible.	I am able to keep myself invisible by an exercise of will-power — an exceedingly exhausting job — and I can keep you invisible.
7. Finally he found it, a few feet from the ground, he could just reach it.	Finally he found it—a few feet from the ground — he could just reach it.

Capital Letters

	INCORRECT	CORRECT
1.	He is working with sterling computers ltd.	He is working with *Sterling Computers Ltd.*
2.	He is a *ph. d.* in English.	He is a *Ph. D.* in English.
3.	Besides *hindi* he is also learning *bengali*.	Besides *Hindi* he is also learning *Bengali*.
4.	Come on a *tuesday, mondays* are bad for me.	Come on a *Tuesday Mondays* are bad for me.
5.	Delhi is on the banks of river *yamuna*.	Delhi is on the banks of river *Yamuna*.
6.	I'm yet to see the *qutabminar*.	I'm yet to see the *Qutab Minar*.
7.	The *mahabharata* and the *ramayana* were by far the most popular serials on television.	The *Mahabharata* and the *Ramayana* were by far the most popular serials on television.
8.	On our last tour we visited *rome* in *italy*.	On our last tour we visited *Rome* in *Italy*.
9.	He did not know that *i* was in the room.	He did not know that *I* was in the room.
10.	I read that report in the *pioneer*.	I read that report in the *Pioneer*.
11.	Have read *the crime and punishment* by Dostoevsky?	Have you read *The Crime and Punishment* by Dostoevsky?

12. The city has many temples   The city has many temples
    dedicated to different *Gods*.   dedicated to different *gods*.
13. Trust in *god* alone.   Trust in *God* alone.

☞ NOTES

1. The first word of a paragraph or after a full stop begins with a capital letter.
2. Proper nouns which are the names of people, places, countries, natural features such as rivers, begin with a capital letter.
3. The first word of a sentence, written in inverted commas, begins with a capital letter.
4. Initial letters, written alone, are written in capitals.
5. Words used in special senses begin with a capital letter.

18

OTHER MISTAKES

INCORRECT	CORRECT
1. The stench in the room made her *ill*.	The stench in the room made her *sick*.
2. He fell *sick* two days before his departure.	He fell *ill* two days before his departure.
3. You must write out your application *with* ink.	You must write out your application *in* ink.
4. When will you *return back* from your trip abroad?	When will you *return* from your trip abroad?
5. My father has *left* smoking.	My father has *given up* smoking.
6. No one thought he could sell his car *for* such a price.	No one thought he could sell his car *at* such a price.
7. I *saw* a dreadful dream last night.	I *had* a dreadful dream last night.
8. We could *make* a goal only in the second half of the game.	We could *score* a goal only in the second half of the game.
9. What is the *fresh* news this morning?	What is the *latest* news this morning?
10. *Good night,* sir, I've been sent to receive you.	*Good evening,* sir, I've been sent to receive you.

INCORRECT	CORRECT
11. She *resembles with* her mother.	She *resembles* her mother.
12. Will you *recommend for* me to the principal?	Will you *recommend* me to the principal?
13. This collection *comprises of* six stories.	This collection *comprises* six stories.
14. He is known to *shirk from* work.	He is known to *shirk* work.
15. He has *ordered for* ten copies of this book.	He has *ordered* ten copies of this book.
16. Who is expected to *accompany with* you on this trip?	Who is expected to *accompany* you on this trip?
17. We *reached at* the platform soon after the train left.	We *reached* the platform soon after the train left.
18. The principal *emphasised on* the need for discipline.	The principal *emphasised* the need for discipline.
19. I have not yet *joined in* any college.	I have not yet *joined* any college.
20. The mob *attacked on* him from all sides.	The mob *attacked* him from all sides.
21. She *has died* last year.	She *died* last year.
22. *What to speak of* milk there is no water in this house.	*Not to speak of* milk there is no water in this house.
23. I have barely got *passing marks* in Mathematics.	I have barely got *pass marks* in Mathematics.
24. Please help me *open* this knot.	Please help me *untie* this knot.
25. The President's House is a *worth seeing building*.	The President's House is a *building worth seeing*.
26. The Ramayana is *worth reading*.	The Ramayana is *a book worth reading*.

INCORRECT	CORRECT
27. He is *foreign returned*.	He *has been abroad*.
28. His watch *goes two minutes fast*.	His watch is *fast by two minutes*.
29. Shalini is a *mutual* friend of Tarun and Stephan.	Shalini is a *common* friend of Tarun Stephan.
30. The *economical* condition of the country is good now.	The *economic* condition of the country is good now.
31. His failure was *owing* to his illness.	His failure was *due* to his illness.